LEFT-HANDED TEACHING
Lessons in Affective Education
GLORIA A. CASTILLO

Traditionally, public schools have had as their main focus the development of cognitive skills. But today many experts in education as well as in a growing number of other fields insist that we must also deal with the affective dimension —with the interests, concerns, fears, anxieties, joys, and other personal and emotional reactions the child brings to the learning situation. When the child is made to feel that his experiences and emotions have nothing to do with the "worthwhile" knowledge the school system intends to set before him, he is being told that he is of secondary importance to the curriculum. In order to teach in meaningful and relevant ways, it is necessary continually to deal with the emotional aspects that are a part of every cognitive learning experience.

In Part I of this book, Gloria Castillo describes a model that allows systematically and predictably for the development of the whole child—his affective as well as his cognitive dimensions—taking account of his readiness-awareness level as well as of his own responsibilities for cognitive and affective development.

While developing this model, Mrs. Castillo came to realize the need for specific material on how to incorporate the student's affective dimensions into the cognitive work of the class-

room. She solicited suggestions from other teachers and from children as well, and the result—a collection of lessons designed to elicit affective responses from the children—is brought together in Part II.

In the final section, one lesson from the affective domain is presented in several cognitive contexts to demonstrate "confluent education" in action. The goal of this book is not to have the teacher use his "right" or his "left hand" exclusively in teaching but to equip him to use *both* hands with equal skill—not to teach cognitive *or* affective lessons but to have cognitive *and* affective dimensions available in each and every learning situation.

THE AUTHOR: Gloria A. Castillo is currently Director of the Elementary Social Studies Project sponsored jointly by the University of California at Santa Barbara and the Esalen Institute. She has been an elementary-school teacher, an educational consultant in confluent education, a supervisor of student teachers, and a workshop leader for various school districts.

Jacket design and photograph by Jay J. Smith

PRAEGER PUBLISHERS
New York · Washington

LEFT-HANDED TEACHING

Lessons in Affective Education

GLORIA A. CASTILLO

PRAEGER PUBLISHERS

New York • Washington

Published in the United States of America in 1974
by Praeger Publishers, Inc.
111 Fourth Avenue, New York, N.Y. 10003

Library of Congress Cataloging in Publication Data

Castillo, Gloria.
  Left-handed teaching; lessons in affective education.

  Bibliography: p. 221.
  1. Education of children. 2. Education—Aims and objectives. 3. Emotions.
4. Senses and sensation. I. Title.
LB1115.C34   372.1'3   73-3679

Printed in the United States of America

To my human teachers

Janet Lederman
Robin Montz
Aaron Hillman
Sherry Carty
and all the children

Contents

Preface
and Acknowledgments

Traditionally, public schools have had as their main focus the development of cognitive skills. But today many experts in education as well as in a growing number of other fields insist that the development of cognitive skills is not enough. They say that we also need to deal with the affective dimensions of the child—his interests, concerns, fears, anxieties, joys, and the other personal and emotional reactions he brings to the learning situation. When the child is made to feel that his experiences, his emotional being, the affective part of him have nothing to do with the "worthwhile knowledge" the school system intends to set before him, he is being told that he is of secondary importance to the curriculum. In order to teach the child in meaningful and relevant ways, it is necessary to blend the cognitive with the affective domain and to seek continually ways of developing the emotional issues that are a part of every cognitive learning experience.

But when I undertook such a search, I soon discovered that there was very little material available on how to incorporate the student's affective dimensions into the cognitive work of the classroom. According to Richard Jones, one of the few who had done practical work in blending the cognitive and affective domains, "The arrangement of opportunities for these coordinative events to take place in schoolrooms is, of course, work for the teacher's 'left hand.' " [1] He and others had developed the effective domain within the confines of a particular curriculum. But that curriculum was not available in my classroom. Even more frustrating, I could not imagine or develop ways to adapt affective lessons designed around the cognitive content to the curriculum I *did* have in my classroom. A way had to be found to deal with the affective dimensions of the child with *any* given curriculum. So I began to work out my own "left-handed" style of teaching.

After two years of experimentation, I developed a model in order to allow systematically and predictably for the growth and development of the whole child—his affective as well as his cognitive dimensions. For me this also meant being concerned with the readiness/awareness level of the child as well as attending to what the child was to be responsible for in terms of cognitive and affective development. That model is described in detail in Part I of this book.

While developing the model for teaching lessons that fostered the growth of the whole child, I became aware of the need to have affective lessons—lessons specifically designed to elicit affective responses from the children—explicitly available so that I could use them again as well as share them with others. The children spontaneously created affective lessons, which I wrote down after they had worked through them. Other teachers offered more ideas. Gradually the collection grew. It has now been brought together in Part II of this book.

Few attempts have been made to relate these lessons to cognitive content. Each teacher in using them will have to make his own arrangements for coordinating them with the cognitive content he has available. Each teacher will then have multiple opportunities to work with his "left hand."

Ideally all learning should be a blending of the cognitive and affective. When such blending occurs, we have "confluent

[1] Richard M. Jones, *Fantasy and Feeling in Education* (New York: New York University Press, 1968), p. 199.

education"—education that allows the child to develop his emotional abilities along with his intellectual abilities. In the final section of this book, one lesson from the affective domain is developed in several cognitive contexts to show how confluent lessons can be developed. The goal of this book is not to have the teacher use his right or his left hand exclusively in teaching but to equip him to use both of them with equal skill; not to teach cognitive *or* affective lessons, but to have cognitive *and* affective dimensions available in each and every learning situation.

Many, many people helped me in writing this book.

First were those who gave me support and guidance along the way: my principal, Robert Pearce, who allowed me opportunities for experimentation; Bud Robinson, who spent many mornings giving me much-needed encouragement; and Dr. George I. Brown, who made the Ford-Esalen project available to me.

Then there were all the teachers and student teachers who were willing to field-test these lessons and give me their suggestions on how to improve them. Many freely shared their own ideas. Carolyn Bogad developed the original "Make Me" lesson (p. 144). Susie McCall gave me the idea for "The Angry Sock" (p. 215). Others gave me the beginnings of a new idea or helped me work out an idea to a logical ending.

Finally there has been my editor, Gladys Topkis. Without her guidance and support in finally bringing this book to its present state I would have given up long ago.

GLORIA A. CASTILLO

Goleta, California
September, 1973

LEFT-HANDED TEACHING

Lessons in Affective Education

GLORIA A. CASTILLO

1
A Personal Approach to Confluent Education

When I began teaching, I was sure I had all the answers on how to become a great teacher. I was young and energetic, and had just been graduated from a reputable "teacher training" college. I knew how to teach, which at that time meant that I could pick up a teachers' manual on any subject, read explicit directions, and, by following those directions, teach the children. I was sure of what to teach, for there were adequate guidelines set by the state and the local school district. All I had to do was teach from the books. I did, and I did it very well according to all those who evaluated my work.

And yet, at the end of that year I had a vague, empty feeling about what had gone on in that class. The highlights of the year, upon reflection, had been the days when we broke away from the prescribed activities and went off exploring something spontaneously, as we did on the day we had a discussion on policemen after one boy told us that the police had come to his house to take his father to jail. Of course, we didn't stay off course very long because there was always the material that had to be covered by June, and the only way to cover it was to march through the textbooks page by page. There wasn't much time for anything else.

Each year the empty feeling grew. Something had gone

wrong on my way to becoming a great teacher. All I had were questions. Where do I want to go in teaching children, and how do I get there? What do I want my children—for these children are mine for the time they are with me—to come to value? What do I want them to understand about themselves, about me, about other people and other things in their world? How do I want them to relate to their total universe? To what do I want them to be inclined to commit themselves?

Of course, I did not have the answers to these questions, but at least now I realized that my empty feeling, my concerns, centered upon the children and not the curriculum. Knowing this, I explored ways of using more of what the children brought into the classroom with them. I rearranged the schedule in order to provide a time when no curriculum would be presented. This was to be the time for the children to direct and control their learning activities.

Again, something went wrong. The children and I were very uncomfortable in this time period. For one thing, I kept expecting the principal to drop in and ask me to account for what was—or was not—going on. I'm sure the children kept expecting me to "drop in" on them and demand the same thing. We tried different things, such as having small group discussions, listening to records, or reading stories. Nothing very interesting or exciting seemed to happen. I imagine I had a harder time with the period than the children did, because even though I wanted it to be a time for them—their development, their growth, their pleasure—I kept wanting to put it all into some kind of structure. But the children had a double standard to work under. The period had to be free and open and structured and constructive at the same time. After a month of this double bind, we were all relieved when I admitted that I was not ready yet to give the children much time away from curriculum or in student-directed activities.

I took over again. This time I began each session with a program. I set the theme of the motivation and gave the children a way to follow through with it. For example, when we studied plants in science, I used that time period to read them a story about leaves and give a lesson on how to make a leaf print. This led to how to do art "rubbings"—coloring over various textures in the room. When a child finished a print he was pleased with, he was encouraged to write a story about it.

I realized that in order for me to let the children work on their own, every child had to be doing something. So I set out to teach or allow the children to do all kinds of things—run the tape recorder, play a record, set up an art project, take the roll. Some were so obvious and easy it is ridiculous to speak of teaching them, but until then I had always thought *I* had to do these things. Little by little, I could allow for more transaction and interaction between myself and the children, letting them know how I felt as they moved around in the room, asking them how they felt about what was going on in the room. Everything was centered on the materials and experiences that collectively could be called the curriculum. For the first time, when the children failed to develop and grow as I expected they would, I looked for the shortcomings or errors in the structure of the class, not in the innards of the children.

That experience was a time of discovering my own expectations and demands as a teacher. I learned more about myself and how I was in the classroom. I discovered my need for structure, boundaries, control. I also discovered ways to give it up once in a while. Little by little, I gave more of that time back to the children. It was also a time for the development of a commitment to the equal worth of all the children and hence to the importance of each child's development and growth, whatever his so-called native capacities. I found that this time period led to much personal growth for me and the children. I also became aware of an urgent need to learn so much more—everything and anything I could about how to teach.

Through the books I read, I realized that the whole educational world was dealing with the very issues I was struggling with in my classroom—namely, the ultimate goals of education:

What understandings, values, and commitments do we want to teach our children? I gained support and drew ideas from leaders in the field of humanistic psychology, such as Rollo May, Abraham Maslow, Carl Rogers, and Sidney Jourard.

At the same time I became involved in the Ford-Esalen project. Esalen Institute was founded to explore the potential of human existence. It does this through a program of workshops and seminars, drawing from humanistic psychology as well as from modern dance, sensitivity training, Eastern religions, and physical education. The Fund for the Advancement of Education of the Ford Foundation provided Dr. George I. Brown, Professor of Education at the University of California at Santa Barbara, and Esalen Institute with a grant for a "pilot project to explore ways to adapt approaches in the affective domain to the school curriculum." The project was thus an attempt to renew the central tradition of Western education—education for the whole man. Its focus was on assembling various approaches to affective learning from the activities in Esalen's unique workshops, conversations with people attending Esalen, reading published materials, and examining them to determine which of these approaches might be appropriate for the classroom. The staff members of the project would then try out the most promising affective approaches with our classes in an appropriate curriculum context and report our results at the monthly meetings. From that year-long examination of affective experiences and experiments in blending them into the cognitive curriculum already available in the classroom, we began to approach curriculum in new ways. The term "confluent education" emerged from our experience, meaning "the integration or flowing together of the affective and cognitive elements in individual and group learning—sometimes called humanistic or psychological education." [1] Confluent education allows for intellectual, emotional, and physical learning.

[1] George I. Brown, *Human Teaching for Human Learning: An Introduction to Confluent Education* (New York: Viking Press, 1971), p. 3.

Although it was not necessarily anticipated beforehand, the techniques and methodology of Gestalt therapy were to play a very important part in the Ford-Esalen project. Both Dr. Brown, the project director, and Janet Lederman, one of the staff, were experienced Gestalt therapists. The late Dr. Frederick ("Fritz") Perls, the founder of Gestalt therapy (or "refinder of Gestalt therapy," as he called himself), was also in residence at Esalen during that time. He would often talk to us informally and expressed great interest in what we were doing. We spent time with him in actual Gestalt therapy sessions, and then he supervised as members of the staff took over the leadership role and conducted Gestalt therapy techniques with other members of the group.

Although we played the role of Gestalt therapist, it was the technique and methodology of Gestalt therapy, not the experience of being a therapist, that we took back to the classroom settings. Gestalt therapy starts with *what is*. It relates the context to the content. Together they form the Gestalt, the whole. The Gestalt approach pays attention to the obvious, to the utmost surface. What was obvious was that we were all teachers in our classrooms even though we were other things in other places.

For example, one tenet of Gestalt therapy that I found especially useful in the class was that of awareness, of myself, my world, my feelings, my fantasies. Awareness leads to being in touch with the environment. Awareness can also lead to new cognition. When I become aware of something, I may discover a need to learn more about it. In the classroom, I worked to develop the children's awareness and used that with their readiness level, their ability to assimilate new cognition, to stimulate their learning activities, striving continually to expand their awareness and their cognitive skills.

While on the project, I was introduced to a new kind of time —the "here and now." This second. This second. Gestalt therapy uses this technique to establish a continuum of awareness. This continuum of awareness is very simple and, like most truly simple things, is difficult to grasp—just be aware from second to second of what is going on, of ongoing experiences, actual touching, seeing, moving, doing. Nothing exists except the here and now. Whether I remember or anticipate, I do it now. Having this new sense of time, an awareness of now, is like adding a third dimension of time. It is the difference between monaural and stereophonic sound. It is the feeling of space I get when flying in a light aircraft. Having a here and now in the classroom allows for a whole new time space, and that space is all life and living.

The specific aim of Gestalt therapy is for the patient to mature, to grow up, and that means to take responsibility for your life, to be on your own. That includes being in the here and now and simply being willing to say "I am I." Fritz Perls describes responsibility as *"response-ability: the ability to respond, to have thoughts, reactions, emotions in a certain situation. Now, this responsibility, the ability to be what one is, is expressed through the word 'I.'* " [2] Just as the concept of the here and now opened up a whole new range of time, so response-ability opened up a new set of alternative ways of being for me. To me the "i" in responsibility stood for "I should." I should teach Johnny to read, I should be creative, I should have a marvelous way to teach something I find boring, and on and on. This is a great way to trick myself out of here and now. It takes me out of the present moment into a world of fantasy. I spent a great deal of my time and energy attending to my so-called responsibilities, my shoulds. But by truly focusing on what I was responding to, my response-ability, I became more accepting of the here and now and also found that I was more open and available to meet my responsibilities.

These two Gestalt tenets were my major focus for the entire year of the Ford-Esalen project. They were not easy concepts

[2] Frederick Perls, *Gestalt Therapy Verbatim* (LaFayett, California: Real People Press, 1969), p. 65.

for me. Over and over again I went to the meetings to seek advice and help from the group. Staying in the here and now was new for me. The new meaning of responsibility confused me profoundly. Until I had an exercise I could put myself through, I had to ask questions of others to know what was happening to me. Try this with me:

"At this moment I cannot be responsible for anything except myself, which includes . . ." My list goes like this: "At this moment I cannot be responsible for anything except myself, which includes sitting here, putting my ideas down on paper." (This also says, "At this moment I cannot be responsible for your reading this.")

This exercise, repeated over and over, helped me to develop an acceptance of the here and now, a willingness to be in the here and now, a faith in the productivity of the here and now. It gave me an entry into that third dimension of time. It also gave me a way to deal with my responsibilities, because at first I felt that accepting responsibility on Gestalt terms was too self-centered, too hedonistic. But gradually I discovered that it was not a negation of responsibility, not a negation of my yesterdays and expectations of tomorrow, but rather an efficient way for me to become aware of what I could and could not do. I cannot live yesterday or tomorrow today. I cannot live any life other than my own. The only moment of life I have is now. I was beginning to realize what Fritz Perls meant when he later wrote: "Authenticity, maturity, responsibility for one's actions and life, response-ability and living in the now, having the creativeness of the now available, is all one and the same thing. Only in the now are you in touch with what's going on." [3]

As a classroom teacher, one issue I faced was that I could not take responsibility for dull, meaningless materials that had to be covered in the year. What I was responsible for was the presentation of the content in those materials. This changed the focus of my energy from the materials to the presentation of lessons

[3] *Ibid.*, p. 52.

dealing with that content in a variety of ways. First of all, I went to my administrator to determine exactly what content and which materials "had" to be presented. I found that many materials did not have to be presented at all. They were there for my use if I wanted them, but I could use other materials and resources for teaching the required content if I chose to do so. I listened to other teachers talk about materials that presented content in interesting or exciting ways. If someone had a good idea on how to present something, I either made arrangements for him to teach it to my class (while I taught

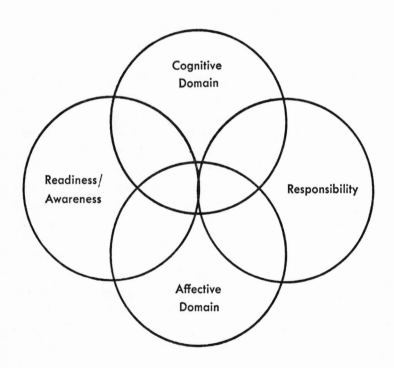

something else to his class) or tried out his idea myself. Sometimes I gave the material to the children and let them present it in their own way. Finally, after much experimentation, I developed a strategy, a structure, or a model for my presentation of classroom materials.

I began by defining a space, setting the essence of what I had to teach and what I wanted to teach into some kind of framework that I could move around in, that I could handle with ease. This meant deciding what aspects of education were most important to me. Through this process, I devised a working model that looks like this:

Cognitive Domain: The subject content that is to be learned —intellectual endeavors, ideas, processes, skills, knowledge.

Affective Domain: The emotional content that is to be explored —feelings, concerns, interests, desires, values, attitudes.

Readiness/Awareness: Readiness to deal with cognitive demands —developing skills, ordering ideas and knowledge, building upon what is already known. Awareness of feelings, emotions, body—responding to the here and now.

Responsibility: Being able to carry out the tasks required of the learning situation. Being able to say "I am I."

Confluent Education: The Gestalt, when cognition, affect, readiness/awareness, and responsibility are totally integrated.

This is just a model, a way to present curriculum in a meaningful, responsible way. In reality, when learning occurs, all these parts come together into one meaningful whole. There is no separation between cognitive and affective domains, between thought and affect, between readiness/awareness and responsibility. Although each part of the model will be described as it relates to the other parts, in reality they don't exist independently.

The cognitive domain represents intellectual content for

the year: the what and how of my teaching responsibilities. What am I hired to teach? What are the cognitive goals of this grade level? What materials are available in the form of textbooks, teachers' guides, state frameworks? To begin with, I go over these materials thoroughly. In any unit, any subject, there are so many concepts, so many things to teach, that I have to make choices. From all that is available, I begin by choosing those items that stir some excitement in me. It may be that I disagree with the author's viewpoint, or it may be that I agree but want to add my own information, my experience, to the material, or it may be that I find the material exciting just the way it is. In any event, it is important that I choose to work with ideas that stimulate me. If I am not excited about learning, I certainly cannot get the children excited about learning.

While still in the cognitive domain, I look to the rest of the model and ask some questions of myself. What affective experience can I provide to go along with the cognitive material? What readiness/awareness must the children have to be able to grasp the cognitive concepts that will be presented? What new knowledge will the children be responsible for acquiring? Many of these questions can be answered in be-havioral-objective terms, and in the cognitive domain they can often be taken right out of the textbooks I am working from.

For example, while working on a math unit on geometric shapes, one of the goals is to have the children name and identify a triangle and a circle. An effective experience for primary children would be to have them "become" a triangle. I would ask, "How can you move? Where are your angles? Can you become a circle now? What do you have to do with your body to change it from a triangle to a circle? How can you move as a circle?"

I would provide many opportunities for the children to be-come aware of the angles of a triangle and the roundness of a circle. I would help them to identify other things in the environment that are like circles or triangles. "The clock is round like the circle. The legs of the chair and the floor make a triangle."

In considering the readiness/awareness aspects of the lesson, I might present only one shape at a time for very young children and more complicated shapes if triangles and circles seem too simple for the group. I might also have to allow the children opportunities to "become" objects before asking them to become shapes.

Once I have made my cognitive selection, I move my thinking to the affective domain. This represents the emotional content that will be explored. It is based on the interests and concerns of the children, on their readiness/awareness, on the level of responsibility they can assume, and on the interest and concern elicited directly by the cognitive content I have chosen to work with. It is the affective domain that gives meaning and relevancy to the rest of the program. It acts as the "supercharger," supplying life to the learning situation and energy for working in the other parts of the model.

In the affective domain, I must provide the children with some way to experience the cognitive concepts, or at least some of them. I do this primarily in two ways. One, I set up a situation so that the children can "live out" the experience in the classroom setting. This allows the children to bring their own here and now to the learning experience and provides opportunities for them to touch, see, hear, move. In math, for example, I once read the children a delightful story that illustrated the need for a standardized length when using the term "foot." Then, before issuing rulers, I had each child remove his shoes and socks, step into a pan of washable paint, and then step off six "feet." We compared the various "definitions" of six feet that resulted and discovered differences. We then discussed the mass confusion that would result if each of us used the same term but used a different "foot" to define it.

We imagined how different things would look if each of several men building one house used his own foot as the measure rather than a standard foot. Each child then measured out six standard feet and compared it to *his* "six feet." He then determined how many more of his feet he would need in order to measure the same as the standard six feet. From there, I pointed out that a ruler is much easier to handle than a true representation of a foot and gives each of us the same definition of the word, at least in the mathematical sense. Later I discovered that this "lesson" had repercussions throughout the year. Often children would discover on their own that two or more of them might be using the same term but defining it differently, and that it was this difference that was causing difficulties between them, not a difference in beliefs, values, or judgments.

The second, and perhaps more difficult, way of working in the affective domain is to have the child imagine how living out an experience relates to his real world, his here and now. This is more difficult because it requires both dealing with the the imaginary setting and bringing it back to the child's real world. There is an abundance of good materials available for getting the child into imaginary settings. However, most of it stops short of adding the child's here and now to the experience. Take the classic "store in the classroom." A child may spend weeks moving about in a make-believe store. Certainly he has a wonderful time with it, and a great deal of mathematics gets reinforced by the selling and buying that goes on. But how much more valuable the store would become if it were brought back into the child's life by providing him with a wide range of opportunities for discovery of self, particularly by asking him "now" and "how" questions: "Now what are you doing?" "Now what are you feeling?" "How do you experience that feeling?" "Who else is in the store with you now?" "How do you feel about his being there?" "How is the store like other places you know about? "How would you like to change the store? Now change it." The possibilities are limited only by available time and possible limiting cognitive concepts. As before, there is so much that can be taught, it is necessary to make decisions.

Some of the questions I would explore are: What rules did you need to keep the store working? How did you know that? What happened when those rules weren't followed? How did you feel then? What do you need from a store? What do you need in order to buy things? What happens if you need or want something and you don't have money or stamps? How did you feel as owner of the store? How did you feel as a worker? An older child, in the fifth to eighth grade, can deal with issues that are current in stores today—rising food costs, the effects of strikes or boycotts, the creation of vacant downtown areas by movements of people, the problem of consumer information, truth in labeling, and so on.

It is necessary to find ways to relate the make-believe store to the child's own life; otherwise it remains at a simulation-game level. The modern supermarket is something that directly affects the life of the community it serves. Studying it affectively can help even a primary child begin to grasp what it means to live and grow up in a democracy with a capitalistic system. It can be another means for him to learn and discover how to cope with twentieth-century ways of life.

Take the specific cognitive goals presented in teaching materials and look for ways to express them in terms of values, concerns, feelings. For example, in reading, a typical objective in the teachers' manual is to evaluate a character in a story. A child can role-play the character and then go on to explore ways in which he himself is like and unlike the character. He can answer all or some of the following questions: How did you feel being that character? What could you do as that character that you cannot do as yourself? What do you do that is like what the character did? What do you do that is different? What else might you be if you were that character? The affective dimension of the lesson consists of allowing for the child's exploration of the emotions available in him that are evoked by the cognitive experience of reading the story.

The affective domain is the heart and soul of the learning experience, just as the cognitive domain is the thinking, intellectual part. They are directly interrelated. The cognitive domain stimulates the affective domain, and, once the child is involved in affective experiences, new cognition arises. In the affective domain, I look to the other parts of the model and again ask questions. What readiness experiences, if any, must I provide in order for the child to have the cognitive experience? What awareness must he have to experience the affective experience, the feeling, sensing, moving part of the lesson? What do I want the child to become aware of while doing the experience? After the experience? What is it that I want him to take responsibility for and about as a result of the affective experience?

From these questions, I move the focus of my thoughts to the readiness/awareness space. This represents those lessons that will be required when introducing new cognitive or affective concepts. We have long been familiar with readiness concepts at the cognitive level. What level of readiness must the child have in order to be able to grasp the cognitive concepts? Is there vocabulary he must understand, clarify, or define? What must he be aware of at the cognitive level? From this, I plan a cognitive-learning program for him. Perhaps I will have to do a great deal of work in this area before moving on.

I then ask the same kinds of questions about the readiness/ awareness of the affective domain. If I want the child to experience something, what must he be able to do to be able to experience it? What do I want him to be aware of? Are there steps to be taken before he can come to that awareness? For example, if I should want a child to respond physically to something that tastes "bitter," he must first of all know how bitter tastes in relation to other tastes. He must have the vocabulary to understand what I want him to do. He must have skills to represent bitter in a symbolic manner, and he must have enough imagination to represent that taste by moving his body in a way that symbolizes bitter for him.

All too often I find that the child has been educated out of his senses, and it is only at rare moments that he will have his emotions available for classroom use. This is what led to the development of the readiness/awareness space in the curriculum model. In the beginning it was a time of day specifically set aside from the rest of the school day for the development of awareness of the here and now, awareness of emotions, and of ways to express that awareness. It was a time when I explored new ways, words, and methods of getting and staying in touch with myself and the child and allowing the child to do the same. It was a time for going through a learning process designed to free the effective domain—mine and the child's— for classroom use. After a while, this was no longer a set period in the day. It became an ongoing process, getting to know what was happening to each individual and what was happening in exchanges between individuals.

The readiness/awareness space is vital for confluent lessons —lessons that integrate cognitive and affective components of learning. Until now in my planning, all of this has gone on in my head, is in and of myself. When I begin to move my ideas into the classroom, it is paramount that I take a good look at where the child is. Initially, I must become aware of what each child is ready for, then take the necessary steps to allow him to be open to new experiences, both cognitively and affectively. Before having the child paint with his feet, for example, it might be necessary to do some preliminary work to get him to feel comfortable about removing his shoes in the classroom or allow himself to step into a pan of paint. This task might be handled by discussions of being and getting "messy," as well as by allowing him multiple opportunities to make a mess. In the cognitive domain, I might have to do more than this one activity in order to get the child to understand and appreciate the need for uniform measurements, if that concept did not "take" in a single experience.

It is in this phase of developing my lessons that I need to use all my skill and ability to stay "tuned in" to the children and what is happening to them. This is the place where I choose either to follow my lesson plan fairly closely, because the children are where I thought they would be when I was planning it, or to abandon it and deal with a whole new set of ideas, because of the instant feedback I have coming to me from the class. It is here that I, as the teacher, make the most discoveries. The cognitive material is already planned for me by curriculum experts. Affective experiences will be influenced by what the cognitive concepts are. In both areas, I do a great deal of selecting. Of all that I *can* teach and do, what I actually teach and do for any one unit is my decision. But as soon as I begin to implement that decision, as soon as real children are added to the teaching and doing, a whole new experience begins to emerge. Until now I have been planning the learning experiences, I have been "the" teacher. Now enter the children —and there are as many teachers as there are people in the room. We all enter the lesson, which then begins to take unique shape and form because all of us are there. It is no longer the lesson I thought up. I give my knowledge, my experience, my planning to the lessons. But it is the children who give direction, movement, life to it.

For me, this is the true art of teaching. A machine can teach children factual information faster and perhaps at less cost than I can. But there is no way that a child can breathe life into that machine. When "learning" from a machine, he might just as well be a dog, an ape, a robot, or another machine, pushing the correct buttons. It is this readiness/awareness space that helps me to be an artistic and not a mechanistic teacher. The cognitive domain can be programed. It is also possible to program the affective domain, and more than one company is doing just that. There are programs available that deal with the affective domain from the standpoint of being a teacher or parent. They include manuals that have daily procedures to be followed. These programs do not take into account where any given child or group of children is at a particular point in time. They are concerned with presenting affective experiences in a step-by-step sequence. The adult, textbook in hand, is in control of the affective experience. Other programs are designed for use by the children. They too fail to take into account where the children in a given group might be. They present a wide range of human experiences—feelings of love and hate, acceptance and rejection, etc.—in a sequence that makes sense from an adult point of view but may be very inappropriate for specific children. But I know of no way to program the readiness/awareness of a child. Certainly there are general guidelines in this area, but one must there with the child in every sense, responding to him, learning from him, in order to provide him with a continuum of awareness.

It is in this area that I determine whether or not the structure of the learning environment is right for the child. If he does not do what I expect him to, I examine his readiness/awareness level in both the cognitive and the affective domain. Once, when teaching from the social sciences, I was having the class deal with the concept of the group. I had the children form groups and had planned various activities and tasks for them to perform while in those groups. Right away, as soon as they formed their groups, I discovered that they experienced a great deal of difficulty communicating when there were more than two people in the group. Rather than continue with my plans, I began to give the children opportunities for self-awareness in a group, focusing primarily on their own experience: Choose two people you feel comfortable with. Talk about the best day of your life. Now choose two people you do not know very well and talk about a frightening experience. What did you experience in the first group that was different from what you experienced in the second group? Were you different? How? What was different? What was the same? What changes occurred while you were in the groups?

Once they became aware of themselves and what was happening to them, the children began to be aware that a group was a collection of "I's." There were comments like, "I just sat in our group." "I waited for someone else to take the lead." "I had some good ideas for this group, but someone else was always talking." They also learned to communicate with each other in more meaningful ways. They then went on to develop the group concepts that were presented in their social sciences material. As often happens, it was through the affective, experiential phase of the lesson that I was given the opportunity to observe and experience the readiness/awareness level of the group and make adjustments in my planning in order to be with the children. It was also in this area that I was able to observe how the children were, and were not, taking responsibility. They could handle the cognitive concepts of a group quite well. They "knew about" groups. However, they were having difficulty experiencing "being" a group.

A new question emerges from readiness and awareness: "What do I have available?" Asked in relation to the cognitive domain, that question means that I want to check my store of required skills and information. If I want to involve the class in a discussion, to use a simple example, do they and I have the skills we need to have a meaningful discussion, or will I do all the talking and they all the listening? Do they have enough information about the subject to engage in a discussion, or is the topic too strange to them? Do they share a vocabulary with which to communicate with each other? Do they know how to listen to each other? What cognitive skills do I have available in order to deal with my emotions and feelings?

When asking "What do I have available?" in relation to

the affective domain, I want to check on my emotions, my fears, my expectations. What am I responding to, what need am I seeking to satisfy? It is not possible for me to know what any other person has available, and so this part of the question is addressed to myself alone. When the children enter the discussion, their responses provide me with some knowledge as to what they have available. Their responses give me further information, further ways of knowing how to extend what they have available to them in the learning situation.

Often when I ask teachers "What do you have available?" the answers are textbooks, resource personnel, books, other teachers, etc. All these things are "out there." They are important, too, but in order to have meaningful curriculum, it is vital to have self-involvement first. Involvement cannot come from, or be left to, others. The first thing a teacher must have available is himself. This may seem an elementary statement, but meaningful curriculum demands that the teacher be actively involved in *his own* development and learning. He must know how he responds to change, to each now, from second to second. He must know how he responds to confusion, to love, anger, joy, and grief. He must be aware of how he responds when he is threatened. He must be aware of his defense mechanisms and of when he is using them. It is necessary for him to become his own critic, for him to know when he is saying "I won't" rather than "I can't."

Try this. On a piece of paper, make a list of the things that usually begin with "I can't. . . ." I can't teach this new math. I can't understand why Paul is so disruptive. I can't do a good job when I have too many children to teach. Now write them over again, beginning each with "I won't. . . ." Feel any difference?

A teacher must become aware of how he feels when children respond. Which responses are comforting, which ones cause him alarm, distrust, uneasiness? What responses do those feelings elicit at that moment? Are any other responses available or possible? He must ask himself endless what, when, where, and how questions. He must avoid asking the traditional "why" and thereby avoid rationalizing and explaining.

A critical aspect of readiness/awareness is the teacher's own readiness to accept the change that confluent lessons can produce. He must become aware of how he personally is as children respond. If he is fearful of letting children explore their own emotions or state their feelings in terms of "I," he must be content to let the children stay with cognitive content only. There may be many good reasons for responding that way, for not allowing children to be aware of what is happening to them, for not admitting what is happening at any deeper level. But the teacher must also be aware that this response does not allow the child to mature, to grow up, to learn to stand on his own, to rely upon himself rather than on the teacher.

A teacher may experience moments of great anxiety if he lets go of some of his old "shoulds" and explores the possibilities of the here and now, the creativity and productivity of the now. It may be reassuring to know that recent research shows that most people are more creative when they are slightly uncomfortable. Too much frustration seems to inhibit creativity, but a considerable amount of anxiety can be borne when the individual who experiences it feels secure within himself.

It is necessary for a teacher to look to himself to discover how secure he is, how he functions both in and out of the classroom. What kinds of expectations does he have when he begins a learning situation? How determined is he to actualize those expectations? It has been my experience that with confluent lessons anything can and does happen. Sometimes I have chosen an activity that unexpectedly provoked so much laughter that I abandoned the goal of the lesson to explore laughter—what makes us laugh, what does laughter say, how can laughter help us to avoid our feelings, how does it show our feelings, etc. Sometimes even with the children's cooperation the lesson falls apart. It does not fit and so has no meaning at that moment. Sometimes everything works according to plan, and sometimes a whole new adventure emerges. How wide a range of experiences will the expectations of the teacher allow to exist in the classroom? How sensitive is he to criticism, especially if it comes from the class? In the lesson I have mentioned, if I had taken the children's laughter as criticism of the planned lesson, something very different would have emerged. As it was, attending to the here and now, listening to the message of the laughter, and directly dealing with that message allowed me and the children a unique learning experience.

In a confluent program, even more than in a strictly cognitive program, learning occurs at irregular intervals. There are bound to be emotional highs and lows. Lessons do not stop at the end of the period if they are meaningful. A tremendous amount of feeling may be generated and set loose in the classroom. What will the teacher do about all this? It is only in the here and now that these questions can be answered. How much control will he need? To try to change the learning environment can be a frustrating experience, and each teacher will have to decide on his own if it is worth it or not.

Observation of the readiness/awareness level of a group leads to the entire area of responsibility. My responsibility is the year-long task of helping the child take more and more responsibility for what happens to him during the year, to grow up, to stand on his own, both in and out of the classroom. This will necessarily be dependent upon the child's readiness/awareness level, his ability to tune in to his emotions, and the state of his intellectual development.

In the cognitive domain, responsibility can be stated in terms of the goals and objectives of the textbook material. What is it that I want the child to know at the end of a unit? What factual information should he have acquired?

What new knowledge should he master in the unit? At the affective level, responsibility means admitting and accepting at a personal level what does or does not happen to and for each individual. For example, "I am doing math." "I am fooling around." "I am drawing a picture." Let me illustrate this by the example of teaching about groups.

From the text, I learn the over-all cognitive concepts of a unit. These are usually stated in very clear terms. In this example, these concepts included: the definition of a group, the structure of a group, the function of a group, the norms of a group, and the diversity of groups. In planning the presentation of the unit, I am careful to include opportunities for the children to master these cognitive concepts. It is usually fairly simple to determine whether a child has done so. The most common way of doing this is to give a test of some sort. In this domain the child's responsibility is to know about groups, and this can be stated in terms of behavioral objectives: I can give a definition of a group, I can describe what a group looks like, what different groups do, what group norms are; I can name different kinds of groups.

Looking at the affective domain, the responsibility shifts from cognitive concepts to doing or experiencing. It is a personal acceptance of behavior and feeling, both negative and positive. I feel I belong to this group; I do not feel I belong to that group. This feels like a group to me; that does not feel like a group to me. I want to belong to that group, so I act in this way. I feel good when I am in this group; I do not feel good when I am in this group. When I am in a group, I affect the group in this way. When I am in this group I am powerful; when I am in this group I do not feel powerful.

The responsibility space is where I as the teacher can see what the child is doing, what he is taking responsibility for, regardless of subject area. It is also the time and place to provide learning experiences that will allow for the continuing development of responsibility. Once the child can experience himself, and then groups, within the classroom setting, I have him explore ways in which groups outside the classroom are the same and ways in which they are different. In this area, I return to the readiness/awareness space to continually broaden and expand the child's concept of himself and how he is in ever-expanding, changing situations. How am I when I am alone? How am I in this small group? How am I in the total group at school? My family group? My community group? My state? How am I an American? How am I a human being? This brings me back to: How am I?

Attending to responsibility is vital in making learning confluent. It directly or indirectly provides for experiences that allow the child to assume responsibility for his learning. I generally start with lessons aimed at self-awareness, because only someone who knows what is happening to him will be able to tune in to what is happening to others. In a classroom I expect a great deal of learning to occur as a result of the presence of other children, other adults, others' ideas as presented in books, etc. All this must move into the child's awareness for the development of responsibility. When each child assumes responsibility for what happens to him to his full capacity, when he can choose that which will give him the most satisfaction, when he can move from one appropriate response to the next, smoothly and easily, then teaching and learning are together in one meaningful whole, with the teacher and the child learning from and teaching each other equally.

Many teachers are alarmed when I speak of a child's having responsibility for himself. But it is the child who does or does not learn, read, do math, cooperate, sit quietly, play vigorously, etc. I cannot be responsible for him in that final step. This does not mean that I can allow the child to do anything he wants, whenever he likes. I do not believe in allowing children to be only where and what they are. To teach is to show the child that more is possible. I feel that I have something to teach, and I want to teach it. And as I am engaged in teaching,

I want the child to be engaged in what is happening to him. This will allow for a wide variety of responses. He may just go along with me, or he may become actively involved or he may need additional information or help. I have a structure to work in, the confluent model, and I strive to provide a learning environment that will allow the child to define his own structure, but always within limits. I do not believe that a child wants or needs license. He needs to know that no matter what he does, he will be safe. No matter how confusing things may get, there will be a time of clearing. He needs and wants freedom, and with that comes responsibility.

Children, and adults as well, do not feel much responsibility for things over which they experience no control. Within the space of responsibility, therefore, I try to develop the concept, "I control myself." This is achieved, in part, by asking over and over again, "What are you doing" and "Who is doing that?" It is also developed by enhancing the child's sense of his ability to make himself felt in his world. The classroom is a large part of a child's world, and so it is necessary to give him some of the responsibility involved in creating that world. Even a kindergartner can be invited to share his ideas on "What do you need a teacher to do for you?" There are real things that a child needs an adult to do for him, and at the same time there are many things a child can be responsible for all on his own. People do not become responsible at a certain age. Responsibility involves lifelong learning. It is not a "subject" but an ongoing process.

It is possible to have many levels of awareness and responsibility in the same class at the same time. Even the youngest school-age child can be given his share of responsibility. Consider the following examples.

My mother makes me dump the garbage.
How does she make you dump the garbage?
She tells me to.

Who dumps the garbage?
I do.
Well, could you not dump it?
No. I have to do it or I'll get in trouble. She makes me do it.
How does she make you do it? Does she take you over there and put your hands on it?
No. She makes me, and if I don't, I get in trouble.

I have to be nice to my sister.
Who is nice to your sister?
I am.
Who makes you do that?
I do. I have to do that because if I don't, my father really gets angry, and I don't like my father to get angry, so a long time ago I decided that I would make myself be nice to my sister.

In the first example, the child seems to be very much aware of what his mother does and as yet does not see what he does in that situation. He is like a robot, with his mother the master controller. In the second example, the child realizes the rewards of doing what his father wants him to do. He does not express the hopelessness, the powerlessness, of the first child. He does something he has to do in order to get something he wants. He has some control over the kind of relationships he has with his sister and with his father, and he is aware of that control.

It is necessary to seek ways to permit the child to have control in the cognitive domain also. When a child is permitted to be aware of what is happening to him, when he takes responsibility for what does and does not happen to him, he can and will make the personal translations from the cognitive domain to his own being. A fourth-grade girl brought her math paper to me stating, "I can't do math." I asked her to find *what* in math she couldn't do. It didn't take long for her to discover that what she couldn't do was master a few multiplication facts. She could add and subtract, borrow and carry. She put aside her paper and said, "I need to work on these four multiplication facts." She left the assignment until she was sure of those facts and then completed it in a very short time. Later in the day she told me, "I like math now. I discovered what I needed to learn, and I learned it."

In helping a child to take responsibility and be in control in the cognitive domain, it is necessary to tune in to his readiness/awareness level. If the material is too far removed from the skills he now has, if it is too foreign to his own readiness/awareness level, he will not be able to relate to it. It is important to identify what the child already knows that will help him to master new materials. What else in the curriculum might be related to new cognitive experiences? What activities can the child engage in to test out his ideas? A child at any age can be remarkably adept at designing methods for answering these and other questions that will emerge from cognitive materials. He satisfies his own needs for learning while involving himself naturally and easily in his play and free-time activities. There is no reason he cannot be allowed to do so within the limits of the classroom.

Giving control to children is not easy for most teachers to do. We have been taught by teachers who were in control of us, and we have been taught to be controllers. Experimentation with allowing children to be in control and with various kinds and amounts of control by teacher and class is a necessary part of confluent education.

Each teacher will have to deal with this issue in his own way. No one can take that final step for him. All I can do is to share some of my experiences, some of my successes, some of my failures.

Once a group of teachers was working with this problem, meeting once a week to discuss what was happening. There were reports of everything from complete bedlam to great success. One teacher had nothing to say for more than a month. Then she came in all excited, proudly reporting, "My confluent program has begun. I kept in mind that the worse thing that could happen would be that the whole class would fall apart. I started a lesson and the whole class did fall apart. I got angry but shared my feelings with the class. They were frustrated with me, feeling that I assured their failure with my attitude. We had quite a discussion, and it was very hard for me to listen to what they had to say. We stayed with it and worked out new directions and now we are really moving along together."

Her decision was to face giving up control, to listen to what the children had to offer, and to allow herself to be uncomfortable for a while in order to "move along" with her class. There is a fine line between losing control and giving up control. In this case, the teacher actually gained control by giving up control, by sharing it with the class.

A teacher will have to find ways to discover what his children feel, what they think about when they are not made to think about school subjects, what they do with themselves when they are free. Continuing questions a teacher must ask the learners are: "How do you feel about this?" and "What do you already know that makes you feel that way?" Also, the questions that people always ask themselves, such as "Who am I?" "What can I do about things?" "Who am I really connected to?" "How do I fit into the scheme of things?" must be explored constantly. This may not be easy. Children have learned very well that the teacher is the source of power in the room and that they must somehow say what must be said in words that he will allow. For example, I had been doing morning lessons on taking responsibility for one's actions for about a week when suddenly one afternoon two boys began an all-out fist fight. Before I could stop them, one had a bloody nose and both were in tears, more of rage than pain. Calmly, I asked what had happened. I got the usual, "He started it." Then, thinking back to our morning lessons, I asked, "What are you feeling now?" Since both boys were still obviously upset and quite angry, I was amazed and confused when one replied: "Sorry." I asked, "How do you know that you are sorry?" He answered: "My mother says to say I'm sorry." This child had learned the words he was "supposed" to say after a fight, but he had no words of his own to express the enormous amount of feeling that went along with the act, or, if he had them, he knew that they were not to be used in this classroom.

Then I asked, "What *might* you feel when you are fighting?" This seemed less threatening than "What *do* you feel?" but still neither boy responded. Others in the class, however, were quite stimulated and very willing to share their ideas since they had not, at that moment, been involved in fighting.

This incident gave me a great deal of material to work on. I realized that these boys were not yet willing to go very far in stating their responsibility, assuming that they were aware of what they were doing. Only when the involvement was at a distance could they respond—they could answer such questions as "What might you feel?" instead of "What do you feel?" and "How does someone else feel?" Knowing this, I continued with readiness/awareness techniques. I found all kinds of opportunities to ask "What are you doing now?" and "Who is doing that?" We stopped during regular activities to finish the statement "Now I am . . ." or "Now I feel . . ." When children got into fights or quarrels, I had them talk to each other, not to me, about what was happening now, and not about what had happened earlier. When a child said "I can't," I asked him to say "I won't." In every way possible I helped, and at times even forced, the children to be aware of their own existence in the here and now.

About two weeks after the fight, one of the boys involved delighted me when he walked in from recess and proudly announced: "I had a fight with John. I gave him a bloody nose. I feel powerful. I feel good." By this I do not mean to say that I encourage fighting. But dealing with fights is part of being a teacher, and I do need to know what fighting does for a child so that I can help him find more acceptable ways to get the same rewards he gets from fighting, whatever they may be. So it was necessary to allow this child to experience his power in an acceptable manner. In every possible way, I helped him to become aware of his power to deal with curriculum (e.g., solving math problems), his power to influence others in the class, the multiple ways in which he affected us, and ultimately the power he used on himself to avoid solving his conflicts with his fists.

In the foregoing case, we had been exploring our feelings in general, allowing them to be present in the classroom, and we had been exploring ways of acknowledging those feelings verbally and nonverbally. It was not until weeks later that this boy was able to express those feelings as his own. One cannot just go through a set of lessons and come out responsible. But by listening, tuning in, going back to less threatening responses, leaving more risk and more involvement always available, applying skill, intuition, and knowledge, the teacher can direct lessons that allow for a continuing spiral of taking responsibility, having both more difficult and more easily reached levels equally available for himself and the children. The doing becomes a trying, an experiment with the environment to find out what it is like. There is always something new to be learned, some new awareness, some new way of taking responsibility for one's life to be discovered.

In developing confluent curriculum, I often feel like a "herder," urging children to accept responsibility, checking a cognitive thrust that cuts off affective approaches, turning readiness and awareness into cognition, seeking to achieve a balance in the over-all curriculum, but still allowing myself to go "way out" in any one area if I sense a need or a desire in the children to do so. There is nothing new in confluent education. It is the discovery or rediscovery of the connectedness of things. Often, when I am doing a demonstration lesson or training workshop, teachers tell me, "I've done that before, but usually only in an incidental or accidental way." I readily agree. We have all had the experience of a "perfect" lesson. We know how to be human. It is just that sometimes we forget.

Teaching is a dynamic art that defies being put down and held down on paper. It is as if I have taken one frame from here and one frame from there out of a twelve-year-long motion picture to create a new picture, one that others can see. I have given it a name so that others may know what I am talking about when I speak of it: "A Confluent Education." Just as there is no "typical" child, no sixth-grader, no college student, even though we can speak of such things, so there is no one form of confluent education, no model. My "model" is a way of showing other teachers what I have done in order to help them develop what they can do on their own. It is a way of helping others to get started, something they can hang onto until they are free to let go. Each teacher will have to break down and destroy this model and develop something that is uniquely his. He will have to develop his resources into his own style, his own way of being "confluent," whatever that means to him. His own individuality is what will make his teaching human and confluent, not merely another gimmick, another set of techniques to try out on children. This model and the lessons that follow are what I have to offer in the faith and trust that each person who uses them will continue to develop something that is in and of himself.

2
Lessons in
Affective Education

Twelve units are presented here, each with several lessons. Unit One, "Awareness of the Here and Now," is designed to develop readiness and awareness for the units that follow and should therefore be presented first. The other units are all interrelated and can be presented in any order that looks interesting or exciting to the teacher. Some of the lessons within the units are presented in a recommended sequence, and this is indicated in the introduction to the unit.

Please read all the way through a lesson before presenting it to the children to determine how it fits the readiness/awareness level of your class. If the lesson seems too easy for the class, combine it with one or more other lessons. If it seems too difficult, find places where the lesson can be stopped before the end and still have some closure. Look at the vocabulary used in the lesson to see whether it is appropriate for the class.

There are timing directions in some lessons. These are only suggestions. You will need to be aware of the interest of your class while presenting a lesson to know whether you should pause for three or thirty seconds before going from one statement or direction to another. It will also be necessary for you to decide if an activity should be pursued for the suggested time allotted to it or if that time is loo long or too short.

Feel free to make changes wherever and however you feel they are needed. It is not possible for anyone to know in advance the special needs, interests, and concerns of a particular class.

Not every lesson has specific suggestions for developing the cognitive domain. It is not the intent of this part of the book to bring in all the cognitive concepts that could be developed with the lessons. It will be necessary for the teacher to coordinate these affective lessons with the cognitive materials he has available.

When it seems appropriate, age differences are noted in the lessons. In general "primary" refers to children in kindergarten or first grade, "intermediate" to children in grades 2, 3, and 4, and "advanced" to more mature students. Again, it is not possible to know the level of any one class without being with it, so the teacher will have to decide how those terms fit his particular class.

UNIT ONE
Awareness of Here and Now

Attending to the here and now is not an easy thing for most of us to do. A great deal of the educational process as we know it emphasizes the past or the future, two aspects of the "then and there." We build on concepts developed in the past, and we develop new ones for use in the future.

This emphasis, of course, has a place in education. But the past is gone, and we remember only what we want or have been taught to remember about it. The future is yet to come, and we can only speculate about it on the basis of past experience. We learn only when we are really in tune, when everything comes together. Only the present, the here and now, is real, and it is almost completely ignored in school. It is usually only when a child cannot or will not deal with the then and there—what he already knows or what he will have to know for the future—that we make an effort to discover where he is here and now. Even so, we do this only in order to make the child move once again from the here and now into the then or there, past or future. In a very real sense, we have been, and we continue to allow children to be, educated out of our awareness of the here and now.

Since we are so unfamiliar with the here and now, it is necessary to develop our awareness on a fairly simple level, one that does not involve too much risk. This means dealing with the here and now in its most recognizable form, taking inventory of our present external surroundings, the environment. For example: "Where am I—at school, at a store, in church, at home, on the street? What other people and what things are here with me in this environment? Who or what is available to me?"

When we ask, "What is available?" we ask for a check of the environment to look for what may have been overlooked before, for a response to the here and now. For example, if a child at school is acting as if he's at home, he is responding to a "then and there." An only child may act as if he is an only child in a class of thirty-five. A child with little responsibility at home may resist accepting responsibility for his life at school. In order for him to respond to the here and now, he will need to take in the school surroundings and see what is available in this environment.

In taking inventory of the here and now, ask yourself, "How much of this environment am I aware of? What do I see? What colors? What light and dark patterns? What people? What things? What sounds am I hearing? How much am I taking into my cognition? Is there more or something else available here, or have I adequately assessed what is available?" The answers to these questions can be discovered by repeatedly asking yourself, "What's available here and now?" and checking your answers with your surroundings.

The answers will change from moment to moment. Sometimes the changes will be minute and subtle. Sometimes they will be dramatic. For example, when I'm home alone during the day, what is available to me does not change very much. The light in the room changes, the telephone rings, sounds of birds come and go. But when the rest of my family enters that very same scene, what is available changes dramatically. I have their presence, their conversation, their responses available to me. At first it may be difficult to know if you are in the here and now or in the then and there, the past or the future. But by talking to, being with, and responding to who and what is in your immediate environment you will develop and expand your awareness of the here and now.

More complex and less visible, yet no less vital to an awareness of the here and now, are the internal responses to the external environment. For example: "How do I feel about this place? Am I responding to its distinctive features, or am I responding as if I were in another place? How do I feel about the people and things here? Am I responding to them, or am I responding as if they were other people and other things? In other words, what is happening to me at a personal level, here and now, in this environment?"

When we become aware of the here and now and all it has available, we can see, hear, and respond in ways appropriate to a given time and place. We are aware of our existence in our environment, and we are in control. We are no longer aimlessly molded, formed, pushed by people and things outside of us. Our actions are the result of a choice among the alternatives available to us, and we make such a choice knowingly.

When this happens, we stand on our own two feet, we take responsibility for our self. We do not need to blame the past, outside factors, or other people for our failures. We do not need to disavow our successes. We can accept full responsibility for both.

A child also has a difficult time attending to the here and now. He too has been educated to consider only the "then" as important. He has not been expected to know what is important to him, what is happening to him. He too has to begin to develop an awareness of the here and now on a fairly simple level.

Although new experiences may be threatening, the lessons in this unit are presented in a step-by-step sequence. The first one introduces only one new idea, "Now." The last one deals with all the ideas in the unit. The lessons are arranged so as to build on what is already familiar to the child to ensure his success in becoming aware of the here and now.

The first three lessons deal with becoming aware of the external environment, with who and what is available. The fourth lesson focuses attention on the internal environment. Lessons 5 and 6 are designed to introduce the child to ways of taking control and responsibility for himself. They are reinforcing mechanisms and are to be used throughout the school year.

Beyond self-awareness, the child should be able to explore the possibilities of extending his awareness even farther—to the group, the family, the community. There should be many daily opportunities, in many forms, for the child to respond to "What am I doing now?" and "How do I feel?" This must be an ongoing process, something beyond the lessons contained here, for awareness does not come easily, and each new here and now brings new awareness. Lessons 7 through 11 focus on awareness of others. Lesson 12 concludes the unit by bringing the child back to himself, with greater awareness of what he has available.

All of these lessons have been used with children from primary to advanced levels. Remember to read through them before presenting them to your class and make any changes you feel would be appropriate.

Objectives

To develop an awareness of the present, the here and now.

To discover new and fresh ideas about what is happening now.

To develop the ability to give a verbal answer to "What am I doing now?" and "How do I feel?"

To take responsibility for actions and feelings.

To identify certain peers as "friends."

To differentiate between reality and fantasy.

To increase response-ability to imaginative situations.

To develop an awareness of who and what are available in different situations and settings.

Lesson 1. Now

Everyone sit in a circle with me. I'm going to share what I know about me right now. I am sitting down. I see you looking at me. I can hear my voice. I see Judy come in the room. I hear the heater turn on. . . .

Continue with statements that are true at the moment you say them. Give enough examples for the children to know what is expected, then allow individual children to respond. Listen carefully, helping only if and when it is necessary to remind a child to keep in the present tense. This may be difficult at first.

Lesson 2. Looking

Sit in the circle again. What did you do in the last lesson? What kinds of sentences did you use?

Their sentences had to be true as of the moment, had to be in the here and now, and had to begin with "I," or with "Now I."

What do you see? Be sure you stay in the here and now and begin each sentence with the words "Now I see . . ." Here is what I see now. Now I see my shoes. Now I see the mole on my hand. Now I see my ring. Now I see the window. Now I see the door.

If the children have difficulty recalling the experience of Lesson 1, review it briefly before going on. Again, begin the game yourself so you can set the example. Listen and help each child to keep his observations in the here and now. Also help him, if necessary, to be specific. Have him rephrase statements like "I see the shoes" as "Now I see my shoes," or "Now I see Ann's shoes."

Variation

Sit in small groups. Take turns going around the circle looking at each person in your group. Don't look for anything special—let images come to you. Begin each statement with "Now I see . . ." Let new images emerge from moment to moment, with each person you look at. Don't force anything.

Lesson 3. Touching Now

Sit in the circle again. Look around the roof and see if you can find something in the room that you did not see yesterday. What can you find? Who can find something about himself today that he could not find yesterday? From where you are sitting, show me what you can touch. Touch something of yours that is hard. It could be your shoe, your elbow, your head. Touch something warm. What on you is warm? Touch something on you that is wet. It could be your eyes, your tongue, your lips.

Now, one at a time, move about the room and touch many things in the room. As you touch something, say, "Now I am touching . . . It is . . ." Touch as many different kinds of things as possible.

Examples: "Now I am touching the sink. It is cold." "Now I am touching the window. It is smooth." "Now I am touching the rabbit. It is soft and warm."

If the child moves into statements beginning with "Now I am touching . . ." continue on. If not, review Lessons 1 and 2, reminding him to make statements that begin with "Now I" and are true of that moment. Then help him to focus on touch rather than sight.

Lesson 4. My Feelings

At various times during the day, have the children stop what they are doing and respond to "What are you feeling now? How do you experience it?"

Help each child to give a complete sentence beginning with "Now I . . ."

Help him to become aware of how he is responding to his environment, how his responses change as he experiences change.

Examples: *"What are you feeling now?"* "I am feeling tired." *"How do you experience feeling tired?"* "I have a pain in my shoulders."

"I am feeling hungry—my stomach hurts."

"I am feeling happy—I am smiling and laughing."

A child needs opportunities to develop a vocabulary to express his feelings in specific as well as general terms. If a child says, "I am feeling good," help him to express "good" in other words. What does "good" feel like to him? Get him to restate it, using another word.

Lesson 5. I Am in Control of Myself

Sit in a group.

Who makes you do things?

How does that person make you do things?

What do I make you do?

The purpose of this lesson is to help the child see that he is actually the one who is in control, doing the action. He is the one who ultimately has to take responsibility for what he does even though others have expectations for his behavior. This lesson is difficult for a child who is used to having adults take responsibility for what happens to him. It may also be a difficult concept for you if you often feel overly responsible for what the child does and does not do in the classroom.

When you first ask the child, "Who makes you do things?" listen to his responses without interference, even if you know he is stating partial truths or has different views of life from you.

Examples: "My mother makes me practice the piano. My father makes me rake the leaves. My sister makes me clean up the mess we make playing house. My brother makes me do all of his work. Jimmy makes me get into trouble."

When you ask, "How do these people make you do things?" it is important, again, to listen to the child's reply without interfering. Use his responses to help see that he does what other people want him to do for a variety of his *own* reasons. Help the child begin to see that he alone makes the ultimate decision to do something or not.

Examples: "I practice the piano so I won't get a spanking. I rake the leaves so I can get my allowance. I clean up the mess because my sister helped me to have fun. I don't really do all my brother's work. Sometimes I get into trouble by myself."

When you ask, "What do I make you do?" listen again to the replies without interfering. If the child's responses still indicate a lack of perception that he is in control and has responsibility —for example, if he responds, "You make me do math"—play the following game:

Say, "David, it is time for math. Get your book and do page 34. Now say everything you are doing." It might go like this:

"I am getting my pencil. I am thinking, What is 7 plus 6? I am writing 13. I am doing my math."

Several repetitions of this lesson may be needed before you get clear statements from the child that he is in control of himself. His responses reflect how much control he has had in the past and his awareness of it.

Games to Play with Lesson 5

"I am a robot"

Pretend that you are a robot. You can do nothing unless you are told to do it. I am the "Master Controller." Before you begin anything new, you must be told to stop the former action.

Walk forward. Stop. Walk backward. Stop. Wave your right arm. Stop. Walk forward. Sit down.

If the child does what you say on the last two commands, stop him and remind him that a robot cannot think for himself. Unless he is told to stop, he would have to walk forward and sit down at the same time. He cannot do that.

Give the child a few more clear directions, one at a time. Then choose a child to be the "Master Controller." Help the rest of the class to do exactly what the "Master Controller" says, nothing more, nothing less.

The children can then write a story about being a robot. "How do I feel when I'm being controlled?" and "How do I feel being the 'Master Controller?' " are good topics.

"I am in control of myself: follow the leader"

Stand in a circle. In a little while I am going to ask someone to go to the middle of the circle and be "It." The one who is "It" says, "I am in control of myself, I can jump." He shows that he can make himself jump. Then each one in the circle says and does the same thing. The one who is "It" then chooses another child to be "It."

Discuss "How do I feel when I'm controlled by the whole group? Would I rather be controlling the group or have someone control me?"

Advanced children can do more complex tasks, such as tumbling stunts.

Lesson 6. What Are You Doing Now?

The preceding lessons in a sense are preparations for this one. It is hoped that this "lesson" will continue throughout the day, week after week, through the year.

While the child is at his regular activities, such as social studies, language arts, math, etc., ask, "What are you doing?" At first he may think that he has done something wrong and will stop all activity. Keep questioning the child until you get a complete sentence, beginning with "I." The following are examples of what might happen on the first try.

"Irene, what are you doing?"
"Nothing."
"Who is doing nothing?"
"Me."
"Now can you put that all together in one sentence beginning with the word 'I'?"
"I am doing nothing."

"David, what are you doing?"
"Working on my math."
"Who is working on math?"
"I am working on math."
"How are you working on your math?"
"Quietly, not bothering anyone."
"Who is working quietly, not bothering anyone?"
"I am working quietly, not bothering anyone."
"Now, what are you doing?"
(Quizzical look) "I don't know."
"I see you smiling at me."
"I am smiling at you."

The following are examples of responses the child might give once he is used to responding in a way that reflects his present being.

"I am hitting Philip."
"I am sitting here doing nothing."
"I am reading my book."
"I am scribbling on my book."

This lesson is a way of putting the child in touch with his reality. It also helps the child to take responsibility for his actions.

Lesson 7. I Have Friends

Lie on the floor and close your eyes. Think of a special friend. If you cannot think of a real one, make one up. Look closely at your friend. Is your friend tall or short? Fat or thin? What color is your friend's hair? What color are your friend's eyes? Take a very close look at your friend. Try to know exactly what your friend looks like to you.

Now pretend that you and your friend are going to a special place. How do you get there? Do you run? Walk? Ride? Think of the place you are in now. What are you and your friend doing at your special place? Keep thinking about your friend and what you are doing. Do anything you want to do with your friend.

Now take your friend's hand and lead him home. When you get your friend home, leave him there and come back here and open your eyes. You don't have to hurry.

Look around and see if you have any friends here. What do your friends here look like? Would anyone like to tell us who his friend is? Try to say "I am (say your own name). (Name someone) is my friend."

With older children you may wish to expand this statement to include what the friend does for the speaker. Examples: "I am Chris. Robin is my friend. He helps me learn to play football." "I am Irene. Lonnie is my friend. She makes me laugh."

Lesson 8. I Am Aware of Someone Else

Sit in a circle. Now make statements about what another person is doing now. For example: "Chris is smiling." "Robin is holding his foot." "Lonnie is talking to Irene."

Listen to each statement, making sure that it is true. If the statement is something imagined or assumed, help the child rephrase it.

Examples: Rephrase "Lonnie is telling Irene a secret" to "Lonnie is whispering to Irene."

Rephrase "Sherry is sleepy" to "Sherry is leaning her head on her hand."

Rephrase "Bob is working hard" to "Bob has a red face."

Lesson 9. Choosing a Partner

Form a close circle. Lie down in the circle, feet to the inside. Be close enough to touch each other. Hold hands with the people on both sides of you. Close your eyes.

Now try to find a partner using just your hands. Let go of one person but hold onto the other. If the person you want to hold onto keeps your hand, you are partners. If he lets go and will not keep your hand, he has someone on the other side of him who is his partner.

Open your eyes and, with your partner, move out to form a larger circle so that each pair has its own space. Talk to each other about how you feel about being chosen.

Now look around the room and see someone else you want for a partner.

Say goodbye to the one you have now and find a different partner. Find a space together and spend some time talking about how you feel about being partners. Is this the partner you wanted? Talk about that and how you feel about it. Say goodbye to each other.

Choose another partner. Find a space together and spend some time talking about how you feel being partners. Say goodbye to each other.

Sit all together. How do you feel about choosing a partner? How do you feel about being chosen? How do you feel about not being chosen? How do you feel about getting the partner you wanted? How do you feel about not getting the partner you wanted?

Pair up the children who do not have partners. Let them spend time talking about how they feel about not getting a partner on their own.

From this experience move into a discussion of other experiences that involve choosing partners.

On what basis would you choose a partner if you wanted to do a report? What would you look for?

On what basis would you choose a partner if you wanted to win a ball game?

On what basis would you choose a partner if you wanted help in creating a story?

Lesson 10. Making a Recipe for a Partner

Choose a partner and find out how he is feeling today. What is he thinking about? Find out what he likes to eat. What games does he like to play? What places does he like to go to? What clothes does he like to wear?

Write or talk about a "recipe" for the necessary ingredients to make your partner. For example:

To be Mike,

You need: Short blond hair
>   2 green eyes
>   1 smiling mouth

Add: 1 strong body
>   1 pair of torn tennis shoes

Comb hair, part down the right side, then swish your hands through it. Place the eyes so that they see the sunshine and sparkle with it. To get the mouth to smile, tell a funny story. Be sure you add the torn tennis shoes, or you won't end up with Mike. Mix with 100,000 freckles. Laugh while mixing.

The age and development of the child determine the type of story he writes. A young child may describe physical characteristics only. An older child begins to recognize the personality characteristics as having more meaning. A primary child may only verbalize his recipe, while an advanced child can write it in true recipe form.

Lesson 11. I Have Available ...

Sit in a circle.

Look around and see what you have available here and now. Be aware of the feeling you have available here and now.

Take turns sharing out loud what you have available, beginning each sentence with "I have available . . ."

For example, "I have available a chair to sit on. I have available a warm feeling about sitting next to Robbie. I have available ears to hear the sound of the jet overhead."

Variations

Have the entire group of children tell one particular child what they see or feel that he has available. "John, you have available very strong arms." "John, you have available a quick smile." "John, you have available a ten-speed bike."

With an older class, have each child write what he has available in different categories, such as here and now, at home, on the playground, in peer groups, or in other nonschool activities.

UNIT TWO
Sensory Awareness

Education ideally is an active, interested exploration involving doing, gaining skills, coming to know. Too much of what passes for education is dulling and passive—memorization, compartmentalization, indoctrination. A child is a whole, but we often act as if he were compartmentalized. We teach only one part of the living, functioning, interacting child, his brain. He has more than just a brain, though. He has feelings, senses, and a body as well.

A child by nature is sensitive, interested, and involved in sense play and exploration. Watch a two-year-old meet something new. He will touch it, look at it, taste it, smell it, get to know it. He is into his senses. Formal education all too often stresses the cognitive functions of the child with little or no regard for his sensory development. We teach him non-sense. This subtle opposition to sensitivity creates an imbalance, a loss of feeling, senselessness.

Every human being, in order to mobilize his full potential, must get in touch with all parts of himself and be able to bring those parts together into a meaningful whole. A child needs opportunities to remain, or learn to be unified. He must be able to feel and think, to see and look, to hear and listen. Only then will he be willing to take risks, to be open, to be creative, to learn.

The lessons in this unit are in order of degree of risk-taking and development. The first eight lessons involve the individual child. Lesson 6, "Breathing in Touch," and Lesson 7, "Tension," are reinforcing mechanisms to be used as often as needed throughout the school year. Lessons 9 through 14 involve extending awareness in order to be with others.

There are no correct responses to these lessons except those that the body expresses. Between indulgence and inhibition is allowing—letting go, letting be, being free to permit or draw the line. Give yourself and the children the open possibility to move, act, or stay inactive in relationship to each ongoing experience, each here and now. Observe the children's movements to determine when they have had enough time to experience a given direction before going to the next one. Feel free to move quickly or slowly through these lessons. The point is not to judge but to be aware, to be in your senses, to do what feels good to you.

Objectives

To experience the body and the mind as an integrated unit.
To relax the body in order to move easily and freely.
To relax the body in order to study without excessive pressure.
To be able to relax and enjoy the company of others.
To develop vocabulary to describe parts of the body.
To develop vocabulary to express feelings.
To continue developing an awareness of the here and now.
To continue taking responsibility for actions and feelings.

Lesson 1. Self-Awareness and Physical Awareness

We have been learning to use our eyes and our hands to find out something about ourselves. Today I want to have you begin with something else. Close your eyes. Use your tongue to explore the inside of your mouth. Feel something soft. Feel something hard. Feel all of your teeth. What else can you feel? Feel your lips. How far can you feel with your tongue?

Now take just your fingertips and, still keeping your eyes closed, tap your head. Tap all over your hair. Feel your hair with your fingertips. Feel where your hair stops and your skin begins. Tap your forehead. Feel your eyebrows. Rub them one way, then the other. Feel your eyelids. Feel your cheeks. Feel your nose. Discover where it stops being hard, and where you can wiggle it. Feel your breath as it goes in and out of your nose. Feel your lips. Feel your ears, inside, around, outside. Feel your jaw. Open and close it as you feel it. Feel your neck. Now put your hands down and feel your face with your mind. What does your face feel like? Now, with your hands go back to any part of your face you want to touch again and explore it on your own.

Encourage the children to close their eyes and keep them closed as long as they can during the lesson. Assure them that if they open their eyes they can close them again when they are ready to do so.

If a child has difficulty closing his eyes, engage in some readiness activities such as: "Close your eyes while I count to three. Now open them. Close your eyes until you hear me tap on the blackboard. Five minutes before recess, close your eyes until the bell rings." In this way you can build up a child's ability to be in the classroom with his eyes closed.

Variation

Do this lesson again and then have the child do a self-portrait of his face only. Have mirrors available.

Lesson 2. Self-Awareness

Lie on your back in your own space on the floor. Close your eyes. Now think of the floor and where you are touching it. I am going to tell you to do some things and ask you some questions. Don't talk out loud, just think of the answers and do what I tell you to do. You will be able to talk later and even tell us other things to do.

Is your head touching the floor? Remember only to think of the answer. How does your head feel? How do your shoulders feel? Are they pressing down on the floor, or is the floor pushing up on them? Feel your hips with your mind. How do they feel? How does the floor feel there? Feel the backs of your legs. How are they right now?

Now, still with your eyes closed, wave your hands in the air. Let them slowly drop to the floor again. How do your arms feel? How does the floor feel? Lift your head off the floor. Hold it up. Slowly let it go back to the floor. How does it feel now? Raise your legs from the floor. Hold them up very high. Slowly let them back down again. How do they feel now? How does your stomach feel now? Now think of the floor again and where you are touching it. Does it feel the way it did when we first began? If it is different, can you feel how it is different? Now, who can think of something we can all do while on the floor?

Again the child may open and close his eyes when he wants to. With a primary child, you might even assure him that you have your eyes open and will see that nothing harms him while he has his eyes closed.

Lesson 3. Right Hand, Left Hand

Make a bracelet out of red construction paper and put it on your right wrist. I am going to ask you to do some of the things you do quite often in this room. To begin, I want all of you to do what I ask you to do using just your right hand. Even if you are left-handed, use your right hand.

Open a book. Turn the pages one by one. Watch and feel your right hand as you do it.

Take out a pencil and paper. Write your name with your right hand on the paper. What is your right hand doing? Where does it begin writing, where does it end? How do you feel writing your name with your right hand?

Use a pair of scissors. Cut something. What are your right hand and arm doing? How do you feel now?

Now use your left hand and do the same things.

Open a book. Turn the pages one by one. Watch and feel your left hand as you do it.

Take out a pencil and paper. Write your name with your left hand on the paper. What is your left hand doing? Where does it begin writing, where does it end? How do you feel writing your name with your left hand?

Use a pair of scissors. Cut something. What are your left hand and arm doing? How do you feel about what they are doing?

If you are right-handed, how did you feel when you did those things with your left hand?

If you are left-handed, how did you feel when you did those things with your right hand?

What things in our room are designed to be used by hands? (Crayons, pencils, scissors, books, dials, knobs, handles, etc.)

Can you find things that are primarily designed to be used by a right hand? (Pencil sharpeners, tuning dials on a TV set, scissors, manual can openers.)

Can you find things that are primarily designed to be used by a left hand?

Imagine how different this room would look if people did not have hands. What might you see? (Doors would not have knobs, pencils might be designed to fit into your mouth, we would have different kinds of clothes on, etc.)

Imagine doing all school activities from a "left-handed" point of view. What might that be like? (We would write from right to left, books would read from back to front, some handles and knobs would be on the opposite side, etc.)

As you go through the rest of the day, be aware of the many things you do with your hands. Find some ways in which our environment is adapted to using hands. You can leave your red bracelets on to remind you to pay attention to your hands.

If you are working with primary children, you may wish to do this lesson in several parts over several days. Focus attention on just the right hand one day, then on the left hand the next. Omit or change any part you feel is too difficult. You might wish to have the child wear a bracelet of a different color on his left hand.

You might also wish to take some extra time with the child who is left-handed. He does live in a right-handed environment, and so it may take him longer to do certain seemingly simple activities. (If you are right-handed, try turning a few pages of this book with your left hand. And remember, you have a great deal more motor skill than a five-year-old does.) Be aware of "right-handed" activities at school and allow him extra time to explore, experiment, and translate them to his left-handedness.

Lesson 4. Right-Left Awareness

Lie on the floor again, finding your own space. Stretch out on the floor, legs apart and arms out from your sides. Be sure you are still in your own space. If you touch someone, move a little. Today you are going to do some things with the right and left sides of your body. Close your eyes.

Now raise your right hand. Have it wave hello to your left hand, which is on the floor way over there. Have the left hand wave back. Raise your right leg. Have it shake at the left leg. Have the left leg shake back. Now have your right hand touch your right eye. Blink your right eye only.

Now blink your left eye. Have your right foot wiggle. Have your left foot wiggle. Have your left ear wiggle. Can you do that? If not, just think about wiggling it. Have your right hand tap your stomach. Have your left hand tap your head.

Continue in this way, keeping the directions fairly simple. Then bring the children to a sitting position and have them talk about things they do with either of their hands or feet. Examples: "I eat with my left hand." "I brush my teeth with my right hand." "I kick a ball with my right foot." "I wear out the toe on my right tennis shoe."

Lesson 5. Right-Left Split

Review some of the things the child discovered he did with his right hand. What did he discover he did with his left hand?

Lie on the floor again and close your eyes. Stretch out in your own space again, being sure not to touch anyone else.

Today you are going to do something that might be a little difficult for you. I am going to ask you to pretend some things about your own self. See if you can do it.

Now I want you to pretend that your whole right side is moving slowly away from your left side. Not too far away. Just have the right side of your head, your right arm, your right hip, your right leg, and your right foot move a little way from your whole left side. Pretend there is a white line down your middle, just the way roads have a white line down the middle of them. Pretend that half of you is on one side of the line and the other half of you is on the other side. Now have your right hand touch your nose. Have your left hand touch your nose. Have your right hand touch your right knee. Have your left hand touch your left knee.

You may wish to do more here, keeping right action on right

side, left action on left side, before moving into the "cross-over," which follows.

Now have your right hand reach over the line and touch your left knee. Have your left hand reach over and touch your right knee. Have your right foot touch your left knee. Have your left foot touch your right knee. Have your right hand touch your left ear. Have your left hand touch your right ear.

Now lie very still on the floor. Think about the parts of your body that were touched. Think about the parts that did the touching. Think about all of your right side. Think about all of your left side. How do they feel now? Now, very slowly, bring both parts back together again. Have them come together slowly and have the white line down the middle slowly disappear as your body becomes one whole body again. Feel how it is to have one whole, complete body instead of two halves. Does it feel different? How? How does it feel the same? When you are ready, slowly open your eyes and look at yourself. Do you see anything now that you didn't see before?

With the child who is still having trouble with the terms *right* and *left,* you might want to have the right hand touch only things on the right side and the left hand touch only things on the left side at first. With an advanced child you can give more complex directions such as, "Have your right foot touch your left knee while your left hand touches your right ear. Have your left elbow touch the floor and wiggle your right foot, etc."

Lesson 6. Breathing in Touch

Lie on the floor in your own space and close your eyes. Take a few moments to experience your body and how it feels on the floor. Now, become aware of your breathing.

Make no effort to change it; just be aware and allow. After a while, place both hands on your upper chest. See that your palms are flat and that the fingers of one hand do not overlap or touch the other hand. Experience the space between your chest and your back. Now, slowly place your hands at your sides. Take a few moments to feel the results of this touch. Next, place your hands on your solar plexus, the area just above the navel, and become aware of what, if any, movement you find there. Again, after a while put your hands on your lower belly, just inside your hip bones. As your hands rest there, shift your attention to your nose and experience the air as it moves in and out. Now bring your hands to your sides and again become aware of how you feel.

With primary children you may want to change the vocabulary of this lesson. The most important thing here is to get the children in touch with their breathing as a way to relax.

This is an excellent quieting activity and is especially good after coming in from rough playground activities. It is also good to use this at the end of a long study session. You can also use it to reduce tension after a test or a testing situation.

Lesson 7. Tension

Lie on the floor. Close your eyes.

Experience how you feel on the floor. Where do you feel the floor pushing against your body? Where do you feel your body pushing against the floor? What parts of you are not on the floor?

Now think about how the inside of your body feels. What parts of your body feel relaxed? What parts feel tense or tight?

Find a place in your body that feels tense. Concentrate on it. Make it feel even tenser. Now suddenly release that tension. Relax. Make it tense again. Suddenly release it again. Relax. Make it tense again. Release it again. Relax.

Now go back to that tense place, but this time do not increase the tension. Just let it be there. Keep thinking about that place, the tension, and how you are feeling. See if you can discover where the tension comes from. Is it just in that place, or does it come from other places, too? See if there is something you can do to release the tension.

Talk about what you experienced.

Tension does not come from outside you. It is something that you produce. Excessive tension can be a message from your body asking you to become more receptive and permissive, to let go and relax. It can also be a warning signal from your body. A headache may indicate excessive tension. It might also indicate dental or other physical problems that your body becomes aware of long before your mind.

This lesson provides another opportunity for expanding the children's vocabulary. They may be unfamiliar with the words "concentrate" and "tension." If that is so, you can give them the definitions or use synonyms that are familiar to them.

Lesson 8. Lifting

Lie on your back with your eyes closed. Slowly bring your knees up toward the ceiling, with your feet remaining on the floor. Experience how your back feels. Now, as if your hips were being pulled straight up by a string, raise your hips and buttocks off the floor. Ever so slowly, raise your entire spine off the floor as high as you can while your shoulders and shoulder blades remain on the floor. Hold yourself there, and then gradually, one vertebra at a time, lower yourself to the floor. Experience letting go to the floor. Feel yourself and the floor now. Repeat, this time raising only the lower half of your back off the floor. Hold, and then be aware of making contact with the floor as you come down. Feel yourself and the floor. Now, barely raise your hips and buttocks off the floor. Hold, and then take as long as you can to lower your back to the floor. Experience how the floor feels now—how you feel now. Slowly straighten your right leg. Slowly straighten your left leg. Feel how the floor is. Open your eyes and sit up.

Lesson 9. Hand Talk

Choose a partner. Lie on the floor, heads touching, feet pointing in opposite directions. Raise your arms over your head and touch hands with your partner.

Have your hands say hello to each other.

Have a conversation with just your hands. How do they feel today? Are they soft, rough, are there blisters or bumps? How else do they feel? Have your hands dance together. Run together. Walk. Jump. Whisper. Tell each other you are happy. Now be sad. Be warm. Be cold. Now just be together with your partner's hands. What do you want your hands to tell your partner? What are your partner's hands trying to say to your hands?

Have your hands say goodbye to each other.

Now sit up and talk to each other about what you did and how you feel about it.

Variation

Have the children do the same type of activity but this time restrict them to the use of thumbs only. Repeat, using other single parts of the body—for example, elbows, knees, feet.

Lesson 10. Tapping-Slapping a Partner

Choose a partner. One of you bend over from the waist, keeping your legs straight. Now the one who is standing begin to tap your partner all over his back. Tap harder. Tap with a firm hand, so as not to sting his back. Be sure you tap every area of the back, taking about three minutes to do this. Now, starting up by the neck, begin tapping all over and down, down, over the buttocks, down the thighs, down the calves, down to the ankles, taking about three minutes to get there.

Change places.

Talk to each other about how it felt to be tapped and how it felt to do the tapping.

We usually think of slapping as a "bad" thing, as a punishment, as a way to hurt someone. However, with children a great deal of slapping goes on that does not fit these categories. Slapping can also be a way of making contact, especially for boys.

Tapping and slapping stimulate nerves, increase blood flow, open every area of the body to be more alive. Use this lesson as an energizer whenever you feel the children's vitality is low.

Variations

Encourage the child to make sounds to accompany his movements and his feelings.

Have the partner who is being tapped kneel on the floor and tuck his head in. This sometimes helps if a short child has a tall partner. It also allows a way for an adult to do this with a child.

Lesson 11. Mirrors

Sit in two rows, one behind the other, all facing the same direction. If you are in the front row, begin to move slowly from the waist up, including your arms and hands. Move slowly. If you are in the back row try to copy every move made by the child directly in front of you. You have about three minutes.

Turn and face in the opposite direction. Again, if you are in the front row, move; if you are in the back row, copy. You have about three minutes.

This is called "mirroring." What happens when we look into a real mirror?

Choose a partner. Stand and face each other. One be the "mirror," the one who copies exactly, and the other be the "doer," the one who controls the mirror's actions. Move slowly so that the "mirror" can follow. You have about three minutes. Change roles. You have about three minutes again.

Now move from your place and return again, with the "mirror" following the "doer." Imagine what it is like to be your partner. Discover what else you can do as "mirror" and "doer."

Lesson 12. Body Rhythms

What noises can you make using parts of your body other than your voice? Choose a sound that you would like to make and go to a space where you can make this sound and not be bothered by some other sound.

Now act like an orchestra, with the different types of "instruments" in different parts of the room. I will choose a child to be the "conductor" and lead the orchestra. One section starts, then the others join in—for example, playing slower, faster, louder, softer.

Some body sounds are: snapping fingers, clicking tongues, clicking teeth, breathing loudly, whistling, sputtering with lips, clapping hands, stamping feet, hitting stomachs for various sounds, slapping parts of the body. Allow the entire class to copy each demonstration.

List all the answers the children offer. You might wish to limit their sounds at first, having them all whistle, or all stamp their feet, or all sputter their lips until they get the idea. Then you can have them combine sounds. You might even tape-record the session.

Lesson 13. Body Building

Form small groups with not more than six children in each one. Now use all the hands you have available and make a house. You have about five minutes to experiment with many arrangements.

Now use all the hands you have to make a school.

This time, make a car. You can use more than just your hands. Use your arms, your legs, your feet, all of you. Be sure that everyone in the group is a part of the finished car. Can you make your car move?

Now change your group into an animal.

What else can your group become? I will allow enough time for exploration.

If the children have trouble realizing what you mean, demonstrate with one group. Have all the children in the group move their hands about in order somehow to represent the structure of a house. This might be done with many hands being the walls, some being the roof, some being the driveway, some being plants in front of the house, etc.

With primary children, it is usually necessary to come to an arrangement using both language and body. With an older class, it is more meaningful if the children are encouraged to do this without talking. It is then necessary to sense what the group is creating to know what each participant's role or addition to the group can be. Doing this nonverbally also reduces the possibility that one individual will take over and direct the entire group.

Lesson 14. A Group Fantasy

Close your eyes and let yourself go on an imaginary trip. You will go to four different places on this trip.

You go out for a walk. It is a warm, sunny day, and you can feel the sun shining on you. You walk to a big hill. It has green, grassy patches on it and places covered with rocks. You climb all over the hill. Even though it might be steep in places, you find you can climb it easily. Now you get to the top. You look out and see a beautiful blue lake.

Climb down from the hill. Run to the lake. Run right into the lake, splash the water all around you. Listen to the sounds it makes, feel how cool it is against your skin. Taste it. Spend some time at the lake. Have a good time with the water. You can swim in it, play in it, do anything you want.

Now come out of the lake and walk on. Again feel the warm sun on you. You are dry now and very comfortable. Now you see a high fence made of wood. Climb the fence. Feel the wood on your hands. Smell the wood. When you get to the top, you look out and see a junk yard. Climb down the other side of the fence and go into the junk yard. Look at all the things there. Over there is an old car. In another place there is some old furniture. There is a pile of bottles and cans in another place. Touch many different things. Listen to the sounds of the junk yard. Let yourself go and discover what else is in the junk yard.

Now you are beginning to get tired. Walk away from the junk yard. Not far away you find a patch of tall green grass. Lie down in the grass. Breathe deeply. Smell the grass. Look, there is a ladybird walking up a stalk of grass. Look at its bright red color and the spots on it. What other things can you see in the grass? Now close your eyes and rest.

When you are ready, come back to here and now.

When you first introduce the child to a group fantasy, be sure to use sensory words and phrases to heighten his imagination wherever possible. Feel free to expand this lesson. Change it as much as necessary to meet the needs, interests, and abilities of your class.

Variations

Start a group fantasy by setting the scene and then let the children direct it. One at a time, a child states out loud what comes next. Each child adds on to the fantasy. Everyone shares the fantasy.

Set a scene such as climbing the mountain and let the child develop the fantasy on his own.

UNIT THREE
Imagination

Each of us has an imagination. Some of us are freer to use our imagination than others, and all of us find it more accessible under some conditions than others. It is an aspect of the learning process that is uniquely human and that most often goes uninstructed in our schools.

Emotions and fantasies can obstruct learning when they are uncontrolled; a feeling or image that cannot be shared is estranging; a feeling or image that cannot be controlled is frightening. Control of emotion and fantasy is essential for the attainment or discovery of knowledge and prerequisite for the formation or invention of knowledge. We need to provide relevant ways for the child to develop, expand, and utilize his fantasies and imaginings as well as his cognitive reality.

Distinctions between reality and imagination are necessary, but it is important to teach the distinctions in ways that do not discourage the imagination.

In the process of learning there should be multiple opportunities for considering alternatives, expressing preferences, and arriving at conclusions independently. All too often we only involve a child in other people's fantasies. The books he reads, the stories he hears, the art he sees are all expressions of someone else's fantasies. We teach him that others are creative, inventive, and knowledgeable. We need to teach him that the same is true of himself.

Reality training as we use it now often puts exclusive emphasis on learning the rules and remembering the facts. It effectively discourages creative or inventive thinking and the exercise of judgment. The following lessons constitute a kind of reality training that does not discourage imagination. The child can learn that there are times for fantasy and times for realism, and that each is good in its own time and way. Just as education based on reality requires time and practice, so does fantasy and imagination development.

We can learn, and teach a child, to be intuitive and expressive, flexible and perceptive, and we can do it without giving up reason, communication, purpose, or emotional control. We can learn, and teach a child, to distinguish reality from fantasy and to discriminate the inner from the outer world without destroying either.

Objectives

To explore the domain of the imagination.

To compare real events with hypothetical events.

To stimulate thinking.

To make more creative use of imagination.

To provide a time and place for fun and laughter in the class-room.

To produce a large quantity of thinking with no "rightness" to it, such as the stories imagined and shared by the children.

To express oneself creatively and appreciate the creative expression of others.

To develop a capacity to integrate fantasy from within with opportunities in the external environment.

Lesson 1. Body Parts

Lie on the floor in your own space. Explore every little detail of your ears with your fingertips. Feel the lobes. Feel the hard parts. Feel in back of the ears. Feel inside. Feel the curving lines. Plug one ear. What do you hear? Plug both ears and listen. What did you hear? Now plug your ears and whisper softly to yourself. What do you experience? Talk softly to youself. What do you experience now? Put your hands at your sides and listen to the sounds of our room. When you are ready, quietly sit up. Share some of your experiences.

Now we are going to imagine some things about our ears. Imagine that somehow your ears moved down to your knees. What would happen if all of us had our ears on our knees?

Imagine that your ears are on top of your head. Now what would happen?

Imagine that your ears are on your wrist. What would that be like?

Where else could you imagine your ears? What would that be like?

When you ask, "What would happen if . . ." questions, accept the child's response with an open mind. If it seems unreasonable to you, ask the child to explain further. It is amazing how many times a child can make creative jumps between fantasy and reality. One first-grader told me that she could hear better if her ears were on her knees because her hair covered her ears. If her ears were on her knees nothing would stop sounds from reaching them. She imagined "many tiny sounds get caught in my hair."

This lesson can be expanded using other parts of the body. Examples: What if your eyes were on top of your head? What if your hands were attached to your shoulders? What would it be like if your head and your stomach were to change places?

Lesson 2. Boys and Girls

The slashes (/) are used to indicate pauses. Do not read the next idea until the child has a chance to do what he wants with the first one. It is important too that the child does this without answering questions aloud during the fantasy so that he does not interfere with any other child's imagination.

The name of this game is Boys and Girls.[1]

Let us imagine that there is a boy standing in the corner of this room./ Let us give him a hat. What color would you like the hat to be?/ Let us give him a jacket. What color jacket shall we give him?/ Let us give him some pants. What color do you want his pants to be?/ Let him have some shoes. What color will you let him have?/

Now change the color of his hat./ What color did you change it to?/ Change it again./ What color this time?/ Change it again./ What color?/ Change it to another color./ Change it again./ Change it again./ What color are his pants now?/ Change the color of his pants./ Change it again./ Change it again./ What color are his shoes now?/ Change them to another color./ Change them again./ Change them again./ What color are they now?/ Have him stand on one foot and hold his other foot straight out in front of him./ Have him stand on the other foot./ Have him walk over to another corner of the room./ Have him go to another corner./ Have him sing a song./ Have him go to another corner./ Have him lie down and roll across the floor./ Have him run around on his hands and knees./ Have him stand on his hands./ Have him sing a song while he is standing on his hands./ Have him run around the room on his hands./

Have him stand on his feet./ Have him jump up into the air./ Have him jump up higher./ Have him jump up and touch the ceiling./ Have him sit in a chair./

Have the chair float up to the ceiling and stay there./ Have the boy sing something while he sits up there./ Have the chair come down./ Have the boy float up to the ceiling without the chair./ Have him float to a corner of the room up there./ Have him float to another corner./ Have him sing "Three

[1] Richard de Mille, *Put Your Mother on the Ceiling: Children's Imagination Games* (New York: Walker, 1967), Game One.

Blind Mice."/ Have him float to another corner./ Have him float to still another corner./ Have him come down to the floor./ Have him say "Goodbye" and go out the door to visit a friend./ Look into one corner of the room and see that he is not in that corner./ Look into another corner and see that he is not there either./ Look into all the other corners, above and below, and find that he is not in any of them./

Put a girl in one corner of the room./ Give her a red hat./ Give her a blue sweater./ Give her a green skirt./ Give her brown shoes./ Now make her hat blue./ Make her sweater yellow./ Make her skirt purple./ Make her shoes black./ Change them to green./ Change them to yellow./ Change all her clothes to white./ Change them to black./ Change them to purple./ Change them to green./ Have her be in another corner of the room./ Have her be in another corner./ Have her sing a song./ Have her be in another corner./ Have her float up to the ceiling./ Have her turn upside down and stand on the ceiling./ Have her walk all around the ceiling looking for the boy who was there before./ Have her look in all the corners up there and find that he is not in any of them./ Bring the boy back and put him on the ceiling with the girl./ Have them standing on the ceiling playing ball./ Put another boy and another girl on the ceiling with them, and have all four playing ball./ Put some more boys and girls on the ceiling, and have them all playing ball./ Turn them all right side up, and put them on the roof of the house./ Put them in the play yard at school./ Make twice as many of them, and have them all shouting./

Make a new crowd of boys and girls on the ceiling./ Put them on the roof./ Put them in the school yard./ Have all the children shouting and running around./ Look at the ceiling and see that there are no children there./ Put one boy there./ Put him in the school yard./ Put one girl on the ceiling./ Put her in the school yard./

Have no one on the ceiling./ Have it full of boys and girls./

Have it empty./ Have no one on the roof./ Have it covered with boys and girls./ Have it empty again./

Put one child in the school yard./ Is it a boy or girl?/ What color are his (her) clothes?/ What would you like to do with him (her)?/ All right, do it.

What is the name of the game we just played?

Allow the child to complete the game in a way that satisfies him. If he wishes to make up an imagination game of his own, encourage him to go on with it as long as time permits and fun continues. Such spontaneous flights of fancy should take precedence over the game as written. You can always come back to the book, but the child's creative act of imagination must be caught when it happens.

Although this game is written for primary children, the style of writing is of great interest to intermediate and advanced children. They enjoy using it for writing their own imagination stories.

Lesson 3. Mixing the Senses

Allow the child to explore an expansion of his imagination through experiences involving his five senses. A normal, healthy, growing child responds to stimuli that activate his sense organs. But sheer accuracy of perception may be emphasized in classrooms so forcefully that the child is unable to retain his earlier ability to transcend the limitations of adult vision, which typically does not allow for incongruity. The term "synaesthesia," used in normal psychology, means that a specific stimulus may rouse not only the specifically corresponding sensation but also a second sensation associated with the first. In color-tone synaesthesia, for example, the perceiving individual sees color while listening to tone. The chart that follows is designed to encourage experiences of synaesthesia by asking the child to look at his environment with a freshness that is not inhibited by accurate perception. It may well enhance the child's feeling of potency to be able to ignore the contradictions inherent in describing a given sensory impact in terms that pertain to other sense modalities.

	Sight	*Taste*	*Smell*	*Touch*	*Hearing*
Sight		What does red taste like?	What does the sky smell like?	What do mountains feel like?	What does blue sound like?
Taste	How does sour look?		What does sweet smell like?	How does bitter feel?	What does ice cream sound like?
Smell	What does the smell of rain look like?	How does perfume taste?		What do the smells of dinner cooking feel like?	What does the smell of soap sound like?
Touch	How does soft look?	What does a rough rock taste like?	How does silky smell?		What does fur sound like?
Hearing	How does a whisper look?	What does laughing taste like?	What does barking smell like?	How does a siren feel?	

This experience will be enriched by having the objects on hand if possible. However, be careful to keep the experience one of mixed senses. That is, do not permit the children to actually taste the perfume or the rock. If you have a soft object for them to touch and look at, be sure they describe what *soft* looks like and not the specific *object*.

Lesson 4. Situations

Look for curriculum content or personal concerns that are present in your classroom that can be adapted to a class participation story, in which a story is told and various parts are acted out by the children. This requires imagination and creativity on the part of both the storyteller and the actors. The story should center around something familiar to children and it should have have multiple roles so that they can choose among many alternative ways of becoming involved in the story.

Primary class-participation story based on a holiday: Thanksgiving

Tell a story about a pumpkin seed being planted by the farmer. It grows into a vine and produces a pumpkin. The pumpkin is picked and brought into the house, where the farmer's wife cuts it up and cooks it. She then adds the ingredients necessary to make it into pumpkin pie. The pie is baked in the oven. It is then carried out to the Thanksgiving table to join in the festivities and eventually be eaten.

Add as many details as you wish as you tell the story. Use many sensory words to describe colors, smells, sounds. It can take five or forty-five minutes to tell and act out this story. Let the children's interest and imaginative participation dictate the length of the story.

Intermediate class-participation story based on a concern: inoculation day

Begin with the serum being in the needle. The needle enters the skin. The serum enters the body. The body responds to the injection. Different parts of the body have different responses. Eventually the reaction to the serum centers on the spot of the injection. The eyes of the body see the reaction, they communicate a message to the brain. The brain gets the body to react according to the message.

Again, let the children dictate the length of the story. They can even dictate the direction the story will take. If you sense that they have fears about what happens if the injection indicates the presence of disease, continue the story in a way that deals with what might happen next (e.g., being retested, getting further medical care).

Advanced class-participation story based on curriculum: cotton

Tell and act out a story about the cottonseed being planted in an area that allows for proper growing conditions. Continue the story from the fields through the processing in the mills to the final product.

There is a rich source of material in advanced curricula that can be developed into class participation stories. Many different stories can be developed during the year. Once a child has experienced a class participation story, he can present one of his own to the class.

Lesson 5. A Secret Hiding Place

Close your eyes and find a place in your body where you can hide. Imagine that you are very small. How can you get inside your body? Look all around you once you are inside. What colors do you see? Do you hear any sounds? Find several different hiding places in your body. Where else can you hide? Where else? How do you get from one place in your body to another? Find the one place you like to hide in the most. Open your eyes and tell where you are. How does the room look to you from your hiding place? Close your eyes and look around your hiding place again. How do you feel in your hiding place? Slowly, slowly, come out of your hiding place, and join us back in this room.

Let those who want to do so share their stories. Encourage them to talk about how they moved about in their bodies and what the room looked like from their secret hiding place.

After the class completes this lesson and each child has his own "secret" hiding place to go to, you can use this as a quieting activity. When the class gets "up in the air" about something, just ask each child to go to his secret hiding place, stay there for a while, and then come out and attend to the here and now.

Primary children would enjoy hearing the poem "Hiding" by Dorothy Aldis before finding their own secret hiding place.

Lesson 6. Your Name

Write your name. See how much space it takes up on the paper. Say your name. Listen to how long or short it is. Does your name fit you? Are you too big for it, are you too small for it, or is it just right?

Imagine you had a longer name. What would it be? How do you think it would fit you?

Imagine you had a shorter name. What would it be? How do you think it would fit you?

Write some long names. Try them on, one at a time. See how you feel wearing them.

Write some short names. Try them on, one at a time. See how you feel wearing them.

Write your own name again. Try it on again. How do you feel about it now?

Variations

Write other names you have been called—nicknames, pet names, variations of your name.

Say each one to yourself and let thoughts and images come to you.

Have the class form into groups of eight to ten. Have one person in each group be "it" and leave the room. Have the others in the group decide whom they will all talk about. It must be someone in their group. "It" returns to the group and asks questions to discover whom they are describing, but can only ask questions of this sort: What kind of house is he? What kind of tree is he? What kind of food is he? What kind of animal is he? What kind of bird is he?

Example—Possible answers for a tall, lean boy with curly black hair:

He is a two-story house.

He is a palm tree.

He is a celery stalk.

He is a giraffe.

He is a cormorant.

On the basis of this type of information, the one who is "it" tries to identify the person the group is talking about. After the identity of the person is discovered, he has a chance to respond to the statements that were made about him—which ones did he agree with, which ones surprised him, how he feels about how the group sees him. There is no correct response. Each child answers with whatever seems appropriate at that moment. Do not allow the child to ponder. Answers should be quick and spontaneous.

Lesson 7. Games with People

Think of a person you like. What kind of food would he be if he were something to eat?

Think of a person you dislike. What kind of food would he be?

Think of yourself. What kind of food are you?

What would you do with all of those different kinds of food together?

Think of a person you like. What kind of animal would he be?

Think of a person you dislike. What kind of an animal would he be?

What kind of animal would you be?

Close your eyes. Imagine a big green meadow. Imagine yourself as your animal. Be in the meadow. Have the animal of the person you like join you as your animal in the meadow.

Have the animal of the person you don't like join both of you in the meadow.

Imagine all three animals there in the meadow. Create your own story.

Talk about what happened in your fantasy. What did the animals do? How did your story end?

Lesson 8. You Remind Me...

Sit in a circle with four to six other children. Sit so you can see everyone and everyone can see you.

Look at the people in your group. Think about each one and who or what he reminds you of. It does not have to make sense. It can be that he reminds you of another person, or he can remind you of anything in the world. Let images come to you.

Look around the circle and tell each person who or what he reminds you of, starting each statement with "You remind me of . . ." Some people may remind you of many things. Tell them as many as you wish.

Discuss what happened in your group.

Now all come together in one group. Are there times when you respond to someone as if he were someone else because he reminds you of someone else?

When someone reminds you of something or someone else, does that help or hinder you in getting to know him as he really is? How?

Lesson 9. Machines

One of you begin to be a part of a "machine" by making a mechanical movement and a sound to go with it. Continually make the same sound and movement. Others in the group, one by one, will attach themselves to you, each one adding his own sound and movement to complete the "machine."

How does it feel to be the one to start the machine? How does it feel to add your own particular sound and movement to the machine? How do you work together to keep the machine going? What makes the machine stop?

Variation

Work in small groups. Each group make your own machine. Each machine move around the room and meet other machines.

Lesson 10. Paperclips

Sit in small groups with four or five children in each one. Here is a handful of paperclips for each group. Choose a recorder for your group. The recorder is to record each suggestion no matter what it is, while you and the members of your group come up with as many uses as possible for the paperclips.

Examples: "I can use the paperclip to clip my hair back." "I can use it to punch holes in this paper." "I can use it to wire my glasses together."

In five minutes the recorder is to draw a line under all your suggestions, and then continue recording. You have ten minutes to do this.

Now look at your list. Did any patterns emerge? Is there any difference between your answers in the first and the last five-minute period? When was the exercise most enjoyable? When was it least enjoyable? How did others in your group spark your imagination? What did you learn about the members of your group? What did you learn about yourself? If you were to do this again, what would you do the same? What would you change?

Lesson 11. Letter to a Baby

Write a letter to a newborn baby. What would you like to tell this child who has just come into the world? Since he is a baby, he knows nothing yet. You know many things. What do you know that you would like to share with him? What do you know that is important for him to know? What do you know about his world that you would like to tell him? What is it like to live here and now? What do you imagine his world will be like? Sign your name to your letter.

This lesson is done best when the child knows a family with a baby. It can be that one of the teachers has become a parent or a former teacher has a baby, or a child in the class has a new brother or sister. It also helps to make arrangements for a baby to be present in the classroom, if only for a few minutes.

UNIT FOUR
Polarities

Education is a major preoccupation for many of our citizens. It seems that everyone is demanding the right to say what should and should not be happening in our schools; industry, government, universities, parents, and student groups are all voicing demands. Should the school be product- or process-oriented? Should it be more traditional or more innovative? Should the goal of education be survival or prestige? Should we strive to produce the world's greatest scientists or the highest literacy rate in the world? Should our goal be the greatest number of Pulitzer Prize winners or the development of a love of knowledge for its own sake—a passion for knowledge and a pleasure in learning; independence in seeking and using knowledge; an acceptance of learning as a lifelong process of self-development?

Today more than ever the issue is change. But what are we trying to change, and how are we to go about it? The computer-industrial revolution demands that what is technologically possible ought to be done and that mankind should strive for maximal efficiency and output. Unfortunately for the humanness of all of us caught in this revolution, maximal efficiency for the system often leads to minimal tolerance for individuality. Some critics insist that we need to humanize education by paying less attention to the process and more to the persons within it. And so the classroom teacher is caught in a dilemma, a polarity. How and what can we teach? In some ways we must prepare the child to cope with the "real" world, a world in which depersonalization and alienation are the rule rather than the exception. We "should" teach him to become a cog in the production machine. On the other hand, we "should" teach the child to reach his full potential as a unique individual, and we "should" make the classroom environment full of meaning for him. This, of course, means making it the opposite of the "real" world.

There is no clear resolution to this polarity. There are times when we must prepare the child for the system. He will be subjected to a battery of standardized tests so that the system can judge if he is at grade level or working up to his abilities. We cannot ignore that aspect of his "education," even though personally we may disapprove of the principle. At the same time we do not have to, nor can we afford to, devote the whole teaching day to preparing the child to meet the demands of the system. A humanistic teaching approach discerns the needs and demands of the child as well as those of the system and provides opportunities for the expression of both.

Basic curriculum guides offer a wealth of materials for dealing with polarities in subject matter itself. To name just a few, in math there are addition and subtraction, multiplication and division. In English there are units on opposite words. In physical education there are many components that can be looked at as polarities—the desire to win and sportsmanship, skill and drill, personal ability and the ability to be a good team player. In the social sciences there are environment and heredity, physical and nonphysical characteristics, the commonality of all mankind and the uniqueness of each individual. There are many ways of looking at anything; attending to polarities can ensure that at least two views will be allowed and expressed. All too often, we, and the textbooks we use, tend toward a one-sided, simplistic view.

Offered here are lessons in what may be called universal polarities. They all have to do with human behavior, actions, and emotions. As such, they can be taught along with any subject matter, where and when it seems appropriate to do so.

The purpose of dealing directly with polarities is to become more aware of what each of us has available, and also to extend our boundaries. We all have characteristics unknown to ourselves, unexperienced parts, gaps in our self-awareness. We have all forgotten or disowned a great deal of what we know about ourselves, especially anything we might consider to be negative. The goal of an exercise on polarities is to become a more complete individual, containing fewer unknowns, fewer unexperienced parts of the self. There is nothing new in these exercises. They are concerned with rediscovery.

Objectives

To be able to think about a single part of the body and compare it with another single, particular part.

To be able to choose a word that describes you and a word opposite in meaning.

To be able to move in a way that others would describe as aggressive.

To be able to move in a way that others would describe as passive.

To develop the ability to look at yourself from two points of view.

To be able to state resentments and appreciations clearly.

To be able to role-play opposite roles and express how each one makes you feel.

To be aware of sending and receiving nonverbal messages.

Lesson 1. Polarities of Your Body

Lie on the floor. Relax, close your eyes.

Become aware of your breathing. Begin to increase your inhaling and exhaling until you are breathing as deeply and

as slowly as possible. How does the rest of your body feel?
Now shorten your breathing until you begin to pant. How
does the rest of your body feel? Now come to a place in between and rest. How do you feel?

Now become aware of the weight of your body. What parts
are heavy? Where is the heaviest part of all? What parts are
light? What is the lightest part of all?

Become aware of the temperature of your body. What parts
of your body are warm? Where is the warmest place? What
parts are cool? What is the coolest place?

Become aware of the texture of your body. What parts are
rough? Where is it roughest? What parts are smooth? Where
is it smoothest?

Imagine dividing yourself exactly down the middle. Compare the right side of your body to the left side. Take each
part in turn and compare it with its opposite, taking time
for each part.

Imagine dividing yourself at your waist. Compare the top
half of your body to the bottom half in weight, temperature,
texture, and other characteristics that come to you.

Compare what you know about the inside of your body
with what you know about the outside of your body.

See if you can discover other polarities in or on your body.
Take your time. When you are ready, open your eyes, sit up
and join the group.

Talk about any surprises, anything you discovered that you
were not expecting.

Now begin to walk around, paying particular attention to
those parts of your body that surprised you, or the ones that
are newly rediscovered. Be aware of your whole body.

Experiment with the parts you have rediscovered. Give
them a voice, one at a time. What do they have to say to you
and the rest of your body? Have each statement begin with
"I."

"I am your left elbow. I am rough and hard and sharp."

"I am the base of your neck. I am tight and very warm."

"I am your bottom half. I give you support. I take you where you want to go. All you have to do is tell me and I will get you there."

"I am your top half. I make contact for you. I do all the thinking around here."

Throughout the day, continue to be aware of your whole body and all your separate parts. Pay particular attention to any messages you receive from any of the parts.

Lesson 2. Polarities of Your Voice

Speak in a soft, gentle, smooth voice. Say soft, gentle, smooth phrases. Examples: "I love you. Goodnight, dear. Are you happy? That's beautiful." Focus your attention on the muscles of your throat. Be aware of how your throat feels.

Speak in a harsh, grating, sharp voice. Say harsh, grating, sharp phrases. Examples: "Get out of here. Who invited you? Now what do you want? Get lost." Focus your attention on the muscles of your throat. Be aware of how your throat feels.

Gossip about someone you don't like, someone not in this room. Listen to your voice. Experience the muscles of your throat.

Gossip about someone you like. Listen to your voice. Experience the muscles of your throat.

How much range do you allow your voice? Is it quite different in different situations, or is it always the same? Experiment with your voice. See if you can exaggerate its polarities. As you go through the day, become aware of when and where you use the polarities and when you use a voice somewhere in the middle.

When do you use certain voices? Do you have a telephone voice? Do you have a teacher voice? Become aware of your special voices.

Lesson 3. Opposites I

Close your eyes and see how you are right now. Accentuate it. Sit that way, breathe that way, hold every muscle that way. Choose a single word that best describes how you are.

Now imagine that your whole body is that word. If your word is "calm," let your whole body be calm. You might even want to lie down. If your word is "tense," tense every part of you—hands, fingers, spine, legs, feet, and toes. Let your whole body be whatever your word is. Let your word grow, completely filling your body. Now have it shrink until it is barely there. Now let your word and your body change however you want.

Now think of the opposite of your original word. Move your body in opposite ways to become that word. Be that word in every way you can. Let your entire body be the opposite of what it was. Sit that way, breathe that way, hold every muscle that way. Let your word grow until it completely fills your body. Now have it shrink until it is barely there. Now let it change in any way you want.

Be your original word again. Move your body to the original word.

Be your opposite word again. Move your body to the opposite word.

Now find a word in the middle, something between the two you have been using. Let your whole body be that way.

Talk about what you discovered. What were your words? How did your body express them? How did the words change? How did your body change?

Do not be concerned if the child does not use exact opposites for his words. You can take time for vocabulary development later. What is important is that the child experience ways of being opposite.

Lesson 4. Opposites II

Close your eyes and feel how you are right now. Accentuate it. Choose a word that best describes how you are now. Imagine that you can be just that one way; no other way is possible. Be just that word for the next ten minutes while you continue in regular classroom activities. If other moods, other ideas, other words come to you, reject them. Stay with that one word.

Now become the opposite of that word. Be just that word for the next ten minutes while you continue in regular classroom activities. If other moods, other ideas, other words come to you, reject them. Stay with that one word.

Now be a combination of all that you are, using your two words and whatever else you want.

What happened to you when you were your first word? What moods, ideas, and words did you have to reject?

What happened to you when you were the opposite of that word? What moods, ideas, and words did you have to reject?

Which way did you like to be most? What did you like about it?

Lesson 5. Passive-Aggressive

Each of us can have many different ways of being, depending on time, circumstances, and how we are feeling. Close your eyes and think of yourself and these two terms: passive, aggressive. Imagine yourself as passive. What are you doing? Who is around you? How do you feel?

Imagine yourself as aggressive. What are you doing? Who is near you? How do you feel?

Now decide if you are usually passive or usually aggressive, knowing that you are really both. Choose to be the one that you usually are, and accentuate it. Open your eyes aggressively or passively. Now begin to move around the room that way, accentuating how you are in every way possible. Breathe that way. Move that way. Begin to make sounds that way.

Freeze. In slow motion, and staying aware of how you do it, become the opposite. Continue to move.

Freeze. Again in slow motion and in full awareness, become your original word again.

Freeze. Now move in slow motion to how you want to be here and now.

Talk about what you discovered.

Which role was the most difficult for you? How did you feel changing from one to the other? Which role did you like most? What did you like about it? How did you feel when you changed?

Have primary grades respond to being "happy" and "mad" rather than "passive" or "aggressive."

Variation

Follow the same format using high and low energy levels; calm-frantic; busy-bored; any other opposites the children suggest.

Lesson 6. Superior-Inferior

There are times when each of us feels superior to those around him. There are also times when we feel inferior to those around us.

Imagine that you feel superior to all of us here and now. How do you move? Show us. How do you feel? Show us.

Now imagine that you are inferior. How do you move? Show us. How do you feel? Show us.

Choose a partner. One of you be superior, the other inferior. Find a way to stand with each other showing that one is superior and one is inferior. Now the one who is superior tell your partner what you have available by being superior. (Examples: I have a view of the ceiling, I have pride, I have a stiff spine, I have a loud voice.) What can you see from your position? What can you do in that position? How do you feel in relation to him in that position? How do you feel about him in that position?

Now, the one who is inferior, tell your partner what you have available by being inferior. (Examples: I can see no one, only the floor; I have fear; I have stooped shoulders; I have chewed fingernails.) What can you see from your position? What can you do in that position? How do you feel in relation to your partner in that position? How do you feel about him in that position?

Now find a way to be equals. Now what can you see? What can you do? How do you feel about yourself? What do you feel about your partner?

As you go through the day, become aware of when you feel superior or inferior. Ask yourself, "What does feeling superior do for me? What does feeling inferior do for me?"

Primary children may respond to the terms "better than anyone else" and "worse than anyone else." You can explain "superior" and "inferior" if it seems appropriate.

Variation

Follow the same format using leader-follower; boss-worker; parent-child; other polarities suggested by the children or by the curriculum.

Lesson 7. Love-Hate

Stand facing a partner. One will do the exercise, the other will observe.

Close your eyes and imagine a person you love. Begin to

focus on that feeling of love. Let it grow, accentuate it. Where is it located in your body? Does it have a temperature? Does it have a color? Does it have texture? Continue to focus on your feeling of love. Put all your thinking, feeling, and imagining into it.

Open your eyes. Have your partner share what he observed. What did he see you do? What did he imagine you were thinking? Share what you discovered. Where in your body did you feel love? Did it have color, temperature, or texture?

Close your eyes and imagine a person you hate. Begin to focus on that feeling of hate. Let it grow, accentuate it. Where is located in your body? Does it have a temperature? Does it have color? Does it have texture? Continue to focus on your feeling of hate. Put all your thinking, feelings, and imagining into it.

Open your eyes. Have your partner share what he observed. What did he see this time? What did he imagine you were thinking? Share what you discovered. Where in your body did you feel hate? Did it have color, temperature, or texture? How did it feel in contrast to love?

The one who worked will now become the observer, and his partner will do the exercises.

Repeat from "close your eyes and imagine . . ."

Lesson 8. Mixed Feelings

We all have times when we feel two ways at the same time about parents, teachers, brothers and sisters, and others.

Think about a person you have mixed feelings about. Imagine that person is sitting across from you. Tell him what makes you angry or upset, what you resent about him. Begin each sentence with "I": "I get angry . . ." or, "I resent you . . ."

Now tell that person what he should do. Make demands. Begin each sentence with "You should . . ."

It may be necessary to help the child begin his sentences with "You should . . ." Beginning by saying "You should not . . ." somehow makes this part of the exercise less effective, less forceful.

Now tell that person what you like or appreciate about him. Again begin each sentence with "I."
Talk about what you discovered.

With primary and intermediate children, do not make a distinction between liking and appreciating. However, with advanced children, it is important to do just that. If you are to make sense out of your mixed-up feelings, it is important to know that you may dislike or resent *and* appreciate the very same thing. A child once told me that she resented me for holding her to an assigned task for a prolonged period of time, but that she appreciated my doing it because now she is quite good at that task and would never have stayed with it without my insistance. It is difficult to know when the appreciation is real and not resentment in disguise. The skill comes in seeing both the resentment and appreciation.

Lesson 9. Mixed Signals

We have all experienced a "double signal." There are times when someone "tells" you two things at the same time. In some way his words and actions are the opposite of each other, or the tone of his voice carries a different message from his words.

Choose a partner. Deliberately give mixed signals.

Talk to each other about anything you want. Whenever you say "Yes," shake your head "No."

Give your partner a compliment in words, and at the same time deny it by the tone of your voice, a hand gesture, facial expression, or anything else you can think of.

Say something negative to your partner, and at the same time deny it by the tone of your voice, a smile or other facial expression, a hand gesture, or anything else you can think of.

Share your discoveries and techniques with the entire group. What works best for you? What is your favorite way of giving a mixed signal? What mixed signals do you experience most often? How do you know they are mixed? Which signal do you choose to respond to? What would happen if you chose the other one?

Continue to become aware of mixed signals as you go through the day. Become aware of the ones you use as well as the ones that are used on you.

Lesson 10. To Do or Not to Do

Put your arm on your desk. Now try to lift your arm, only do not really lift it. Be aware of how the rest of your body feels. Now this time really lift your arm. Again, be aware of how the rest of your body feels.

Repeat.

Talk about what you experienced.

How is this exercise like other situations in your life? Have you ever experienced yourself exerting more energy *not* doing something than you would exert doing it? The next time you are faced with doing something you don't want to do, experience how much energy you exert in not doing it, and how much energy you exert when doing it.

With primary children, use "working hard" instead of "exerting energy." Ask them to relate this experience to one in which they have worked hard *not* to do a chore.

Lesson 11. Genius/Idiot

Choose a partner.

Roll up a single sheet of newspaper. Each one grab one end of it. You are to pull your partner over an imaginary line between you without tearing the newspaper. If you tear it, roll up another sheet and try again.

Choose another partner.

Imagine your *genius*, that part of you that knows all the answers, knows how to solve problems, can come up with a solution to any given problem. Be that genius as you work to pull your partner across the line without tearing the paper.

Discuss any difference between doing it now as the genius and doing it the first time.

Choose another partner.

Imagine your *idiot*, that part of you that never does anything right, makes mistakes every time, always needs help. Be that idiot and work to pull your partner across the line without tearing the paper.

Discuss the differences you experienced.

Choose another partner. Decide on one of those two roles, the genius or the idiot. Do not tell your partner which you are. Try to pull him across. Try to discover what he is as you are working.

Discuss how you experienced each other.

Continue to choose different partners, trying on one or the other role.

What happened when you were playing the genius?

What happened when you were playing the idiot?

When do you really play the genius? When do you act as if you know more than you really do?

When do you really play the idiot? When do you act as if you need more help than you really do?

When can the role of the genius be useful to you? When could it be harmful?

When can the role of idiot be harmful to you? When can it help you?

This is a particularly good exercise for the child just before he takes an examination. It gives him a way to act out his idiot and his genius. He can then enter the exam at ease, relaxed, and ready to do his best, leaving his idealized genius and his complete idiot aside.

Lesson 12. Paper Structures

Sit in a group with four to six children.

Without talking, each group is to build a structure, using newspaper as the building material. At the end of ten minutes your structure will be judged for height and stability.

Begin to work. Remember, you are not to talk to each other while you work. You can use gestures and sign language, but no words.

Wait five minutes.

Freeze. Think about how you have been working in your group. Choose a word that describes how you've been working, your role in the group. One by one, say your word out loud. (Examples: worker, helper, designer, goof-off, paper folder.)

Now imagine that you are the opposite of that word.

Continue working, again without talking, and in your opposite role.

Wait five minutes.

Stop working on your structure. Compare your structure with others in the room. Which is the highest? Which is the most stable? How can you decide?

What did you discover about yourself? What two roles did you play? How did you work with your group while you were in your first one? How did you work with your group while in your second role? Did you stay in your second role until the end, or did you switch roles again? If you switched, what did you switch to?

What did you discover about others in your group?

It is difficult for a group of children to work nonverbally at building a newspaper structure that is "high and stable." Yet amazing things happen when they do. Very often a group which gets going early in the lesson destroys their structure when told to be opposites, and then proceeds to build it up again just before the time is out. Conversely, a group that has not been able to get anything together builds a structure quite easily while being opposites. This exercise allows the children another way of being, another way to tackle a task.

The process of judging the structures can be a meaningful learning experience for the children. How can the height be measured? Who can be trusted to take accurate measurements? How can stability be measured? What will be the basis of judging stability?

UNIT FIVE
Communication

Effective communication is essential in relating to others. Real communication involves sending and receiving messages, but most of us are primarily concerned only with sending messages. Very few of us can listen without talking, although most of us can talk without listening. The integration of talking and listening is a rare thing. Most of us don't listen and give an honest response but just put the other person off with a question. Instead of listening and answering, we immediately counterattack, ask a question, make a senseless remark, anything that diverts, deflects, dodges real communication. But without communication there can be no contact. We are only isolated and bored.

Communication concerned with receiving a message involves a willingness to understand another person's point of view or way of looking at the world, or perhaps even his unspoken needs and goals. Communication associated with transmitting a message involves much more than organization of thoughts or clarity of speech. It requires sensitivity to the needs, level of comprehension, and receptivity of the receiver. If the other person hasn't received, we haven't communicated.

Most really significant communication between people involves feelings, not ideas, and is nonverbal. In most communication with people who are important to us, we listen as much to the unspoken messages as to the words. Even with people who are not important to us we have an inner ear tuned to nonverbal messages concerning sincerity, dependability, and frankness. We constantly rely on nonverbal feedback from others, but often we are not aware of the nonverbal messages we transmit. We can and must increase our sensitivity to others' reactions, to their nonverbal communication, as well as to our own.

Typically we do not allow the child at school to become actively involved in developing adequate communication skills. We often limit his communication to hours and hours of listening only. But he has more available for receiving than his ears. He needs multiple opportunities for sending messages too. He needs opportunities to develop awareness of and skill in many ways of communicating.

The following lessons deal with blocks in sending and receiving messages, in giving oneself, in making others aware of oneself, and in being willing to be open to other people.

In the first lesson the child may discover that he does not listen very well or very often. But with practice he will improve his skill in listening to another, as well as be provided with instant feedback on his ability to listen and restate what he heard. By continuing through the other lessons, he can begin to develop an "inner ear" for listening. He will explore various ways to listen and various ways to interpret his listening ability. He will be encouraged to use more of what is available to him in any listening situation.

Objectives

To communicate an interest in others.

To be perceptive regarding your effect on others and their effect on you.

To be open, receptive, and interested in the ideas, opinions, feelings, and reactions of others.

To be able to accept constructive feedback or criticism without reacting defensively, becoming hostile, or withdrawing.

To be able to provide constructive criticism, meaningful feedback, support, and encouragement to another person.

To develop the ability to listen to the totality of another person—his body as well as his words.

Lesson 1. Listen, Repeat

Sit in a group of four to six children.

Anyone in the group may say anything he wants to say, but he must speak in a clear, simple sentence.

In order for someone else to speak, he must first repeat what the speaker before him said.

Example:

Speaker A: "I'm going to get some new shoes after school today."

Speaker B: "I'm going to get some new shoes after school today. I am going to help John build his fort."

Speaker C (may be Speaker A again): "I am going to help John . . ."

Strange things happen when you use this lesson. The child gets so intent on listening that he actually forgets what he was going to say—what he "rehearsed." It not only improves listening ability, but also aids in developing precise, clear English.

Lesson 2. Trite Conversation

Choose a partner. Talk to each other, but have a "trite" conversation. Talk of nothing that is of importance to you. Talk about what you ate for breakfast, how to clean your room, anything that seems trite to you.

Come up front in pairs and introduce your partner to the group. Check with each other to make sure that what you say is correct and is something you know about your partner because of your trite conversation, not from former information.

How did you feel having a trite conversation? How did you keep it trite? How did you feel introducing your partner? How did you feel being introduced?

When do other people have trite conversations? When do you usually have trite conversations? (Examples: When I don't know the person very well. When I feel the person isn't really interested in what I have to say.)

Lesson 3. More Conversation

Choose a partner, preferably the same one as in "Trite Conversation." One of you be "A," the other "B."

Alternate talking and listening for five-minute periods. Have "A" ask "B" the same question over and over for five minutes and "B" answer over and over, seeking new answers to the same question. Then "B" asks "A" the same question over and over for five minutes before going on to the next question.

Ask each other the following questions:

Who are you?

What do you pretend?

What makes you cry?

What makes you happy?

How did you feel answering the same question over and over? Which question was easiest to answer? Which one was the most difficult? Did you discover any answers that surprised you? Did your partner say anything that surprised you?

Lesson 4. Kanga Talk

In this story Kanga and her baby Roo have come to live in the forest. The other animals who live there decide to play a trick on Kanga by taking her baby, Roo, and giving her Piglet instead. Kanga goes along with the trick by taking Piglet to her home and pretending he is Roo. Here is what happens:

"I am not all sure," said Kanga in a thoughtful voice, "that it wouldn't be a good idea to have a *cold* bath this evening. Would you like that, Roo, dear?"

Piglet, who had never really been fond of baths, shuddered a long indignant shudder, and said in as brave a voice as he could:

"Kanga, I see the time has come to speak plainly."

"Funny little Roo," said Kanga, as she got the bath water ready.

"I am *not* Roo," said Piglet loudly. "I am Piglet!"

"Yes, dear, yes," said Kanga soothingly. "And imitating Piglet's voice, too! So clever of him," she went on, as she took a large bar of yellow soap out of the cupboard. "What *will* he be doing next?"

"Can't you *see*?" shouted Piglet. "Haven't you got *eyes*? Look at me!"

"I *am* looking, Roo, dear," said Kanga rather severely. "And you know what I told you yesterday about making faces. If you go on making faces like Piglet's, you will grow up to *look* like Piglet—and *then* think how sorry you will be Now then, into the bath, and don't let me have to speak to you again." [1]

How can two people be talking "at" each other instead of "to" each other? Can you think of another dialogue that fits the pattern? Share a similar conversation.

Can you recall any conversations like this between you and someone here?

Can you recall any conversations like this between you and somone you live with?

[1] A. A. Milne, *Winnie the Pooh* (New York: E. P. Dutton, n.d.), Chapter VII.

Listen to how people talk to each other and try to discover the times when they talk "to" each other and the times they talk "at" each other.

Variations

Form small groups. Develop skits demonstrating how people talk "at" each other instead of "to" each other.

Examples: Classroom scene, teacher and child talking "at" each other. In the family car, parents and children talking "at" each other. Older child talking "at" younger child.

Write stories demonstrating examples. Here is one from an advanced student.

Strawberry Shortcake

It was a sunny afternoon in late June. Mrs. Green was preparing supper when Alice rushed in.

"I'm going to be in the spelling bee, Mother. First prize is a new television set," Alice burst out.

"What do you think we should have for dessert tonight, Alice?"

"I hope I win!" she said abruptly.

"What, the dessert?"

"NO—the spelling bee!"

"Maybe strawberry shortcake would be nice."

"I wonder if they have a color set," Alice said questioningly.

"Yes, of course, strawberries have color."

"Mother, you are not listening to me."

"Of course I am, dear."

Lesson 5. Build a Story

Begin telling a story that really sparks the child's imagination. It can be related to a holiday theme, a science or social-studies unit, or one just for fun. After a few minutes, stop and have a child continue the story. Let each child add at least one sentence.

Example: One dark and gloomy night I was in an old haunted house. The wind began to blow. Doors slammed shut, windows creaked. Suddenly I heard a loud crash in the kitchen. I ran in there to see what was happening and what did I see, but a . . .

Variations

Pack your trunk

Speaker A: I am packing my trunk. I am taking a shirt.

Speaker B: I am packing my trunk. I am taking a shirt and a toothbrush.

Speaker C: I am packing my trunk. I am taking a shirt, a toothbrush, and a jacket.

Continue until all in the group get a turn to pack something. If time and interest allow, unpack the trunk.

Do what I do

One child stands in the group and begins a nonverbal activity. (Build a house, prepare a meal, put up a tent.) Others join him in his activity once they imagine they know what he is "saying." They can imitate his motion or join in doing the same task in their own way.

Lesson 6. Talking with Hands

Suppose you couldn't talk. How could you say "Hello"? Do it now, without talking. Say hello to a friend without talking. Say hello to another friend without talking.

Imagine you are angry. How could you show that using your hands and not your voice?

Now imagine you are shy or nervous. How could you show that with your hands?

Imagine you are happy. How could you show that with your hands?

Choose a partner. Say hello to each other using just your hands. Have a conversation with your partner using your hands. While your partner is "talking" try to listen with your hands. Stay together long enough to allow yourselves to have a hand conversation.

Lesson 7. Listening with Eyes

I am going to tell you some things, but I am not going to use words. I am going to use "body English." You are to listen to what I am saying, but you will have to listen with your eyes.

(Look and act very stern.) What am I saying?

(Look very pleased.) What am I saying?

(Act very proud and "stuck up.") What am I saying?

Now you do it.

Say you are a very old man.

Say you are a spoiled brat.

Say you are a very tired, sleepy child.

Say you are very anxious to get my attention.

Say you are angry.

Say you are happy and cheerful.

Say what you are really feeling now.

During the rest of the day discover what a person says with his body and his voice.

Discover when he says two things at once.

Can you give examples of how a person might say two things at once? (Examples: Say "You can sit next to me," but act as though you don't want that person anywhere near you. Say "Stop it!" and smile.

Lesson 8. Nonverbal Statements

Choose a child to be "It."

Have other children in the group come up one at a time and make a nonverbal statement either to or about "It."

You can touch "It" if you wish, hug him, hit without hurting, stroke, pat, etc.

You can imitate "Its" stance, facial expression, mannerism, way of moving.

Encourage the children to express their impressions in any way they can other than through the use of words.

Then have the child who was "It" respond, again nonverbally, to each one who made a statement to or about him. He can show each child his agreement or disagreement, his pleasure or scorn, in any way he chooses except that he cannot use words or cause pain or injury to the child. When he is through with his response he can choose another child to be "It." Help him to be aware of what kind of nonverbal messages he may receive to influence his choice. Did he choose a child who smiled at him? Did he choose a child who waved his hand as if to say, "Me! Me!"?

Lesson 9. Total Listening

Choose a partner. Face each other. One of you is to talk and the other is to listen. As you listen, imitate your partner's facial expression, how he moves his hands, his "body English."

If, when you are the one who is talking, you become speechless or embarrassed, tell your partner how speechless you are, how you feel about standing there face to face embarrassed.

Change roles. The one who was talking becomes the listener. The listener becomes the talker.

Choose another partner.

Repeat several times. Be talker and listener with different people.

Discuss: Who was difficult to talk to? Who was difficult to listen to? Who was easy to talk to? What did he do that made it easy to talk to him? Who was easy to listen to? What did he do that made it easy?

Lesson 10. Imagining Sounds

Sit so that you are quiet and comfortable. Close your eyes. Think of a loud sound that is familiar to you. (A train going by, thunder, sirens, etc.) Concentrate on that sound. Where are you when you hear it? Is anyone else there? What time of day is it? How do you feel when you hear that sound? Where in your body do you experience that feeling? (Stomach, shoulders, back of knees, head, etc.)

Now think of a soft sound that is familiar to you. (Rain gently falling, whispering, leaves rustling, etc.) Concentrate on that sound. Where are you when you hear it? Is anyone else there? What time of day is it? How do you feel when you hear that sound? Where in your body do you experience that feeling? Is it the same or different from the place where you felt the loud sound?

Discuss what you discovered.

You might wish to make the children's responses to these questions into a math lesson by having them tabulate their answers. By doing this, the child discovers that even though his answers are based on his own experience, there are others in the class who share similar experiences.

Lesson 11. TV Commercials

Watch several commercials on TV. (This could be a homework assignment.)

Listen to how the announcers try to persuade you to buy their products.

List advertising sentences or phrases aimed at eliciting an emotional response.

Examples: "A little Accent's like a little love."
"You don't have to be expensive to be good."
"Your friends will agree."
"Score some points the easy way."

Make a list that includes the product being sold as well as the implicit by-product you will get when you buy the product. For example,

Product	*Byproduct*
Cosmetics	Romance
Hairspray	Long, curly, easy-to-manage blonde hair
Margarine	A jeweled crown, riches of a king
Hand lotion	A family enjoying each other, having fun

What effect do these commercials have on you? What do you imagine the people who make up the commercials see as being important to you? What is important to you?

Which commercials "turn you off"? What is there about them that you do not like? What makes you "turn off"?

With older children you can go on to explore the following.

Which commercials do you enjoy? What is there about them that pleases you? Have you ever bought a product because of watching a commerical? If so, did you like the product as much as you liked the commercial?

Be aware of how you are responding while you are listening to and watching commercials. Make notes. Share them with the class.

Lesson 12. Words, Words

Make a list of phrases that everyone uses frequently. For example: "How are you?" "Where have you been?" "Isn't it terrible?" "What's the matter?" "I'll see you later."

Now choose two or three children to work with you.

Divide a piece of paper into three columns. In the first column, list ten of the phrases on your list. In the next column, write what you think the speaker of those words really means to say. In the third column write what you imagine would happen if you were to respond to the phrase with complete honesty. For example: If asked "How are you?" what might happen if you took the time and effort to really tell how you are?

Since everyone uses these phrases frequently in meaningless ways, how do you know when someone uses them and means them? How do phrases like that teach you not to listen to one another?

Try to respond honestly to a meaningless phrase at least once today. Be aware of what happens to you and to the speaker when you do.

Primary children can respond to this orally. You might want them to consider only three or four phrases.

Lesson 13. Twenty Words

Take a piece of paper and a pencil to a place where you can be quiet and comfortable.

Of all the words you know, choose the four words you

think are most important for you to be able to communicate.

Now get into a group of four to six people. Each of you use your four words, and only your four words, to communicate.

Now sit by yourself again. Look at your four words. Evaluate each one. If any of them did not help you communicate, cross them off your list and add more words so that you still have four words.

Now add four new words so that you have eight in all.

Get into a new group of four to six people and use your words. Use only your eight words, even as you form your groups.

Sit by yourself again. Look at your eight words. Again, cross off any words that you did not find useful. Add other words so that you still have eight.

Add four new words, so that you have twelve words in all. Now use your twelve words in a new group.

Evaluate your list of twelve words, making any changes you want.

Now add four new words, so that you have a list of sixteen in all.

Use your sixteen words in a new group.

Evaluate your list of sixteen, making any changes you want.

Add four new words to your list, making twenty in all.

Do not go into a group, but sit by yourself and look at your words. Read them through several times. Let thoughts and images come to you as you read them.

Use those twenty words to write a poem, make a statement, or share an image about yourself. You do not need to use all twenty words, and you can use any of them as often as you wish.

Bring the whole group together. Let anyone who likes read his poem or statement to the entire group.

Here is one such poem written by a sixth-grade boy.

> Less aware I came,
> More aware I go.
> We share thought, trust, love and hope.
> What now is here
> I feel will be elsewhere.
> Less aware I came,
> More aware I go.

UNIT SIX
Building Trust

One of the most difficult things to do is to trust someone else, to give yourself to another person. We can all recall situations when we have trusted someone only to be disappointed, betrayed, left "holding the bag." And yet very little is being taught in classrooms on how to discriminate between healthy and harmful contacts with people. We do not teach the child how not to make the same mistakes over and over again in his interpersonal transactions. Instead we allow him to learn this very important aspect of becoming a self-confident, self-actualizing adult on a purely trial-and-error basis. We do not teach him how to be careful, how to listen, see, think, and feel about the way in which contact with another person affects him. We do not allow him to ask, "How do I feel now? What do I know that makes me feel that way?" If the contact is unpleasant, he is not helped to understand exactly what is unpleasant; thus overgeneralization, stereotyping, or withdrawal may occur. We leave the entire area of how to give and receive trust entirely to chance, and so we also leave the child "holding the bag" when it comes to being able to build trusting relationships.

The lessons that follow are a beginning attempt to bring this important area into focus in the classroom. They are by no means exhaustive. This is one area about which little is supplied by traditional teacher materials. And yet how much trust must be developed in the average classroom for real learning to occur! If learning is, as one definition has it, discovering that something is possible, the bonds of trust must be well established and well developed. Without trust in his peers and his teacher, how can the child be expected to venture out into unknown areas? If he cannot learn to trust others, how can he learn to trust himself?

We teach children to compete with one another, to outperform others, to get better grades, and so on. But what does all this do to their ability to trust? I don't know, but I do know that using lessons designed expressly to establish bonds of trust between children has added a new dimension to my classroom. Competition has continued, but not on a devastating level. Children begin to appreciate one another more, begin to see worthwhile qualities even in those who cannot or will not compete in the usual way.

What are lessons designed to build trust like? Read *Black Beauty* to the children and explore the idea of the trust that exists between man and his animals. Explore multiple answers to these questions: How do you know when an animal trusts you? How do animals act when they don't trust someone? How do you act when you don't trust someone? What do I need to do in order for you to trust me? What do you need to do in order for me to trust you?

Form small groups and have them stand in circles. Each child goes around to each of the others in his group and completes this statement: "In order for me to trust you, you should . . ." And then around again and finish this statement: "In order for me to trust you, I should . . ." And still again, "I trust you when . . . I do not trust you when . . ."

The following answers came from a fifth-grade class:

"In order for me to trust you, you should
 never make fun of me."
 speak to me in a soft voice."
 often smile at me."
"In order for me to trust you, I should

spend time being with you."
do something nice for you."
be as good at baseball as you are."
"I trust you when
you play fair."
you do what I tell you to do."
you are nice to me."
"I do not trust you when you
are mean to me."
are with Marcy."
insist on having everything your way."

Have the children talk about the people they live with and how they trust them. Have them write about the person they trust the most as well as the person they trust the least. They may discover that the one they trust the most is the same person they trust the least. Have them talk about that, too, and how sometimes life is very complex and perplexing.

Play trust games, such as "falling" (Lesson 3) or "trust circle" (Lesson 4). How close to you does the group have to be for you to trust them to catch you? Can you allow yourself to fall farther?

Another useful device is to take a trust walk or a blind walk. Have each child choose a partner, put on a blindfold, and let his partner take him on a sensory trusting excursion. Have the children use that experience to explore the following questions: Whom did you choose for your partner? On what basis did you choose? Which did you like most—being blind or leading? What did you like about it? What did you discover about your partner on the walk? What did you discover about yourself? Imagine being on a blind walk with someone you don't trust. What might that be like? Are there real times in your life when you feel as if you're on a blind walk? (Some experiences related by children are visits to doctors or dentists and riding in a car with a reckless driver.) How do those experiences affect your ability to trust other people?

Deliberately establishing trust is a new area of consideration in the classroom, one that needs a great deal more study. A commonsense reminder before you continue: Don't force any child to participate in any of the following activities. You must trust the child to know what he can and cannot allow himself to do. You can provide the opportunities for him to build his trust, but he must know that he will be allowed to be where and what he is, that he will not be obliged to do anything. It is hoped that the following lessons will provide enough insight for you to continue the development of trust on your own.

Objectives

To learn to "give in," to let someone else take over.

To be able to work cooperatively with others.

To be responsive to personal needs and to be considerate of the needs of others as well as the requirements of a given situation.

To be able to trust others and to gain their trust.

To be aware of and express new appreciation for members of the group.

Lesson 1. Hand Painting

Materials: Fingerpaint paper (large, white, smooth sheets), dry tempera, starch.

On half of the desks, tape down one sheet of paper and place a container with enough starch to cover the paper and another container holding dry tempera.

Choose a partner and sit down across the desk from each other, facing each other.

Clap your hands, shake your hands, rub your hands. Now clap hands with your partner. Shake hands with your partner. Rub hands with your partner.

First, without using starch or color, you and your partner move your hands over your paper together. Explore a rhythm of movement that is comfortable for both of you. Move in a variety of ways. Move slowly, quickly, in jerks, in slides, in taps and in slaps. Find a way that enables both of you to move as one.

Once you are able to move together easily, pour starch on your paper and spread it all around, still trying to move as one. Continue moving the starch around until it begins to get somewhat tacky or the paper begins to show signs of wear.

Now put your fingertips into the dry tempera and add color to your movements. Continue to concentrate on moving together rather than trying to paint something.

Do the movement you like to do the best while moving together. Make that movement all over the paper and leave it like that to dry. The paint will make patterns, and you will have a painting of your moving together.

Lesson 2. Feed Your Partner

Arrange it so that all the children can eat lunch in the classroom together. Have the child choose a partner and sit across from him. Each child is to feed his partner and not himself.

This sounds quite simple but actually it is quite difficult. We are all so used to "taking care of ourselves" that it is not easy to give in and let someone do something like feed us. If there is a child who is reluctant to allow himself this experience, have him just sit with the group and feed himself. He might allow himself to be fed a bite or two by either you or a friend before the period is over.

Lesson 3. Falling

Have the child choose a partner and stand behind him about ten inches away, facing in the same direction. The child in front falls back and lets his partner catch him. In order to really fall, the child in front can't move his feet to catch himself.

Change places so that the one who was falling can now catch his partner. Repeat the process, discovering whom you trust to catch you and who you feel will not be able to catch you.

With a child who is afraid of falling, decrease the distance. With a child who is not afraid, increase the distance to the limits of safety. Let the child define those limits by placing his partner at a distance he feels is comfortable.

Lesson 4. Trust Circle

Once the children are comfortable with falling, have them form small groups of six to eight. One child is in the center, and the others form a close, tight circle to catch the center child as he falls. The one in the center has to keep his feet in one spot and keep his legs and backbone stiff so that the children in the circle can pass him around by moving the upper part of his body from one to the other.

The circle must be small enough so that the child in the center has a short fall and is therefore not too heavy to be passed around. Be sure to stop the exercise before the children get too tired to continue to catch the child in the center.

Variation

Have the children sit in a tight circle on the ground using their feet to anchor the feet of the child in the center. The one in the center holds his feet still and his legs and back stiff. He then falls to the group. The group use their arms and hands held up over their heads and slightly forward in order to pass him from person to person. The one who "drops" him or cannot pass him on then becomes "it" and goes into the center.

This is a great experience. However, it is a strenuous activity and requires strong arms. It should be used with caution.

Lesson 5. Working Together

Take the children to a smooth floor surface. Give each pair of children a large piece of material to work on (double bed sheets are ideal).

Choose a partner. Both of you must stay completely on the sheet and must move from one side of the room to the other.

Choose a third child to join you on your sheet. All three of you must stay completely on the sheet and move from one side of the room to the other.

Have a contest with another group. See which can move in the most unusual way. Which can move fastest?

Have elimination races. Which group is the best team?

Increase the group to four and do the same.

Increase the group size until it gets too difficult to move in a determined direction.

Discuss what happens when you work in a group. What makes a group work? What do you do to make it work? How do you feel when you get the job done? What happens when your group doesn't work? What do you do when it doesn't work? How do you feel when your group is stuck, when it can't move in any direction? How is our classroom like the big group on the sheet? When in the classroom do you work well? When do you get stuck in the classroom?

Variation

Place two children on one sheet and tell them to move in opposite directions. Give them time to work out their conflict. (One solution is that they go first to one end and then the other.)

Lesson 6. "I've Got It and I Want to Give It to You"

Form a circle of ten to twelve people.

One child begins by saying, "I've got it and I want to give it to . . ." (names a specific child). The first child then holds his hands as if he were holding something, goes to the named child, and hands it to him. The next child does the same thing, passing "it" from child to child.

Encourage the children to act out properties of "it" without giving it a label.

Ask questions along the way, especially the first time through the game. For example: Is it heavy or light, big or small? Will it get away if you let go of it?

Lesson 7. Passing Invisible Objects

Sit in a circle. One child passes an invisible, unidentified object to the child next to him. Each child in turn passes "it" until "it" has gone all the way around the circle.

Game 1. Hold your hands as if you had something in them. Pass the "object" to the child next to you, being sure you really give it to him and he really takes it. Be sure you pass the same object you received.

Game 2. Begin passing an "object" as in game 1. When I say "change," the child who has the object is to change it in some way before passing it on. You can change its weight, its size, its temperature, or anything else you think of. Keep the object the same until I say "change" again. Change it several times around the circle.

Game 3. You can say "change" when you pass the object

to the next child or you can say nothing if you want it to stay the same.

Game 4. Each one of you change the object when you take it so that each of you passes something different from the object you received. (Once while doing this game a mischievous fifth-grade boy "ate" the object as soon as he received it. The girl who passed it to him looked horrified and exclaimed, "How could you eat that? It was a leaf with a slug on it!")

Game 5. Take the object passed to you. Decide if you want it or not. If you do, keep it and pass something else. If you don't want what you got, change it and pass that on.

If you have difficulty keeping the object in the group, you have an excellent opportunity to explore what happens to a game when someone refuses to play, what happens to a group when someone refuses to cooperate—how you feel about that person, what that person feels when he does that, and so on.

Lesson 8. I Can Make Contact

Sit in small groups.

Each person look at every other person in the group and think about how you can make contact with that person. Then, one at a time, each child in the group make a direct verbal statement to each of the others in the group, beginning each statement with "I can make contact with you by . . ." "Robert, I can make contact with you by playing football with you." "Sharon, I can make contact with you by smiling when you look at me." "Brad, I can make contact with you by hitting you."

As the teacher, it is important that you do not place value judgments on the statements, particularly if they are negative. Some children are limited to negative means of contact. If this is so, it is important that the child himself, or herself, becomes aware of it. Until he is aware of it, he can do nothing about it.

Variation

I can avoid contact

Exactly the same as "I Can Make Contact," except that the direct statement is "I can *avoid* contact with you by . . ."

Some of the statements may be identical. "I can make contact with you by smiling at you" and "I can avoid making contact with you by smiling at you" may both be true statements, even addressed to the same person.

The purpose of these two exercises is for the child to become aware of what he is doing when he makes contact, and what he is doing when he is not making contact. Smiling may look the same in both cases but it does not feel the same. Confusion and mistrust of others occur when this distinction is not clear.

Lesson 9. I Seem to Be ... but ...

Complete this sentence. "I seem to be . . . but . . ." (Examples: "I seem to be bored, but I'm only waiting." "I seem to be real cool, but I'm only in a cold sweat." "I seem to be letting you have your own way, but underneath I'll never give in.")

Variation

Make statements about each other completing this sentence. "You seem to be . . . but . . ." "You seem to be rough but I know you to be soft too." "You seem to have lots of friends, but you can be lonely too." "You seem to know it all, but you still make mistakes." "You seeem to be shy, but you are friendly."

Lesson 10. I See and I Imagine

Sit in pairs or small groups. One at a time, look at a person and say something you see and then add what it is you imagine because of what you see. "I see you turning red. I imagine you are embarrassed." "I see you smiling. I imagine you are trying to reassure me."

Be sure that the statements that begin with "I see . . ." are actual observations. It may be necessary to restate some sentences. "I see you are nervous" should be changed to exactly what it is that is seen to cause the observer to imagine nervousness—"I see you wiggling around in your chair" or "I see you looking away from me," or whatever it is that can actually be seen. Then, "I imagine you are nervous."

Lesson 11. Giving of Gifts

Sit so that you can see each other. Today you are going to give gifts to each other. Pretend that you have the whole wide world available. The gift can be a real thing or an imaginary one. Look at each person here and see what it is you would like to give him or her. You may want to give something to everyone, or you may find you want to give to only a few. When you have decided what your gift will be, and whom you want to give it to, walk over to that person and tell him or her, one at a time. Begin each statement with the name of the person you are giving the gift to.

"George, I give you a big chocolate cake."

"Susie, I give you a kitten all of your own."

"Bob, I give you a little green man to pick up after you wherever you go."

Discuss what you discovered while doing this lesson. How

did you feel when giving a gift? How did you feel when receiving one? Which gifts did you like? Which ones would you rather not have? How did you deliver your gifts? Did you rush up, drop a gift off, and rush back, or did you do something else? Was it different for different people?

These questions are only suggestions, for when you involve your class in this game the kinds of questions you ask will be those that you feel should be brought to the awareness of the group. In a discussion of what happened, beware of judging it as good or bad. The purpose here is to deepen the child's awareness of himself and others, not to place a value judgment on his activities.

It is important in this exercise that the child uses the name of the recipient of the gift and that he owns the giving by saying "I give." If you hear the phrase "Here is . . ." have the child restate it.

Variation

Have small pieces of paper available on which the child either writes or draws his gift. When he says, "_____, I give you _____," he hands the appropriate piece of paper to the receiver.

UNIT SEVEN
Aggression

"Teacher! Tell Susie to stop bothering me. She keeps pulling on my paper while I'm trying to work." The teacher looks up to see Tim grab a pencil from Bob and race around the room with it. Billy reaches over and socks the boy who sits next to him. When it's time for the class to go to recess, there are quarrels about who gets to take the ball out, with the strongest one imposing his will on the others. There is pushing and shoving to see who can be first in line. Eventually there are children in tears.

That scene is quite familiar to most teachers. Healthy, normal children are often aggressive. Aggression is not necessarily a negative force in the development of a thinking, caring, responsible person. Without it we would never question answers, never seek new ways to express life, never stand up for ourselves. Given rational objects, aggression is healthy. It provides us with initiative, drive, and energy to set out on a task and accomplish it. It is only when this energy is thwarted and directed toward destruction of self or others that neurotic derivations of aggression develop.

If the children exhibit acts of aggression or become aggressive while in the classroom they are typically forced to suppress their aggression. Often they then divert that energy inward, using it to tear themselves down. This only adds to their feelings of frustration, impotence, and inadequacy.

This unit attempts to deal with aggressive attitudes and acts by giving the children acceptable releases for their aggression and by emphasizing rational, healthy forms of aggression rather than irrational and neurotic forms. These lessons help the children to become aware of their aggression and to gain control over what they do with it. Until they can become aware of what their aggressive impulses are and learn to put them to constructive uses, these impulses are certain to be misused.

Obviously children should not be given complete freedom to express their anger. The expression of aggression must be controlled in order to protect the children. The object of these lessons is to teach the children to feel their aggression, to be fully aware of it. How to express it is also taught within the context of reality. This here and now, this time and place, will necessarily temper how aggression can be expressed.

Suppose, for example, that a student becomes aware of a need to feel powerful through his aggressive acts. Once he knows that he is seeking power, he can begin to experiment with acceptable ways to feel power. For example, he can learn to feel powerful by sawing a board in half rather than by punching someone in the nose. His awareness will necessarily require a testing, a trial-and-error period. Even if his trials are successful, his aggression will still be aggression, but it will have been put to useful tasks and will not have been destructive to him or others. It will have been expended as the situation demanded and allowed, and so it will not need to accumulate into an explosive volcano.

A teacher who cares about the total child will make a time and a place for aggression in the classroom. It does exist, and it does serve a purpose for the child who is using it. The child must have opportunities to become aware of all his emotions. Dealing with aggression in the classroom gives the child another way to face himself honestly and openly. If he learns to identify and to accept his aggressive attitudes and acts, he can be in control of them. He can learn to use them for his growth and development, not just as forces for self- and other-destruction.

Objectives

To take part in a discussion of negative feelings and how they have effects on living with others.

To be able to experience anger where and when it occurs.

To know when and where anger can be expressed, and to express it at appropriate times and places.

To be able to describe negative feelings that emerge while playing games.

To be able to remain stable in the midst of stress and strain.

To develop a safe way to take on another student and engage in physical contact with him.

Lesson 1. Pushy Behavior

Each of you write a direction for what you consider to be a "pushy" behavior on a sheet of paper. Write it so that someone else can act it out. Examples: "Act tough. Show off. Be childishly rude. Do something outrageous." Place your pushy behavior in a box and draw out another one. Role-play it. Let the class guess what role you are playing.

What pushy behavior do you see occurring in this room? What do you see that makes you call it pushy? What is your favorite way of being pushy? Do you have a favorite way to be pushed? Make a list of all the ways you are pushed about during the day. Make a list of all the way you push others during the day.

Lesson 2. Pushing

Choose a partner. Face each other about two feet apart.
Raise your hands to shoulder level.
Reach out and place your palms on your partner's palms.
Keep your hands at shoulder level and push against each

other's hands. Push as hard as you can. See if you can push your partner back.

Variations

Choose a partner and demand whatever you want from him without thinking about what he may feel or want. Change roles. Talk about how pushy the demands were and how you felt about them.

Choose another partner. Repeat as before.

Now look around and find someone who really bothers you. Push him. See if you can push him back. Be sure you stand face-to-face and begin with your palms together at shoulder level.

What did you discover? Whom did you enjoy pushing? How far did you want to push your partner? Were you strong or were you a pushover?

Have the child stand with his right side against his partner's right side. Have him push with his other side.

Have the children stand back-to-back and push with their shoulders. Have them stand back-to-back, bend over, and push with their buttocks. Have them experiment with other ways of pushing.

This lesson can be introduced in Physical Education or during a play period. However, it is hoped that once the child knows what to do he will be allowed to use it often. For that to happen you must define safe limits. The limits will necessarily depend upon safety precautions appropriate to the area. When playing outside in an open or grassy area, for example, the limits might be between first base and home plate on a baseball diamond. In the classroom, only one pair of children can push at a time in an aisle between rows of desks, and they can push only the length of the row.

This lesson is very effective with a class that pushes and

shoves at every chance. By allowing a time and a place for the behavior, you can get a lot of it out in the open to be dealt with honestly, or to be over and done with. You might find it beneficial to allow the children opportunities to do this activity several times a day. Even a young child can offer tremendous resistance in this stance. You should join in this game too. There may be several children who would relish the chance to take on the teacher.

Lesson 3. Pulling

Sit in a double circle facing a partner. Join hands and lean back, pulling against your partner, but keeping in balance. How far back can you lean?

Stand on your knees. Lean back, still holding hands, keeping in balance. What do you have to do to keep from falling?

Stand up. Put your feet together close to your partner's feet. Hold hands and slowly lean back. How far can you let yourself go and still keep balanced?

Change partners. Repeat this sequence several times with different partners.

How well did your partners work with you? How well did you work with your partners? Did you have any difficulty working with anyone? If so, what made it difficult? What did you do about it?

Each child should have some success with this even if it is only at the sitting level. If you find a child who consistently pulls his partner over and if the partner complains about it, try to make the child aware of what pulling his partner over does for him. (For example, it proves he is strong, makes him fail early in the game on purpose so he doesn't have to fear failure while really trying, lets his partner know that he does not want to work with him, demands control of his partner, etc.)

This is also a good lesson for teacher involvement. Try to maintain a standing balance with a child you enjoy. Now try it with a child who irritates you. Do you feel any difference?

Lesson 4. Silent Scream

Close your eyes and imagine that you are going to some quiet, comfortable place by yourself.

Think of something that bothers you. Imagine that no one is near you, no one for miles around. Continue to think of the thing that bothers you. Let it bother you more. More. More.

Now, silently scream. Open your mouth and scream silently as loud as you can. You are alone, no one will hear you.

Now scream as loud as you can out loud. Loud. Louder.

Now think of the thing that bothers you again. See if you can imagine doing at least one thing about it that would stop it from bothering you. Imagine doing something real and possible to lessen the force of what bothers you or to stop it.

When you are ready, open your eyes. Discuss what happened.

Lesson 5. Living with Others

Sit in a circle. Close your eyes.

Imagine that you are talking to someone in your family, someone who has made you angry. Tell that person how he made you angry. You are doing this in your imagination so no one can hear you. Make your statements explicit. "I get mad when you tear my books." "I get angry when you leave a mess for me to clean up."

Now tell the imagined person what you like about him or her. Make your statements explicit. "I like you when you read to me." "I like you when you clean the bathroom after you use it."

Who in this room makes you angry? Again, in your imagination tell that person how he makes you angry.

Now in your imagination tell that person what you like about him or her.

Open your eyes and look around. Look at each one of us here. Share anything you wish to share.

If the child makes a negative comment about someone at home or at school, have him go on to state something he likes about that person as well. Help the child to keep his comments very specific, avoiding "it," "they," and "she." Get the child to take responsibility for his anger. Have him change "It makes me mad . . ." to "I get mad . . ." Using "it" projects his anger outward to some unidentified thing. By using "I," he can internalize his anger and begin to integrate it with the rest of him. By using a specific language, he will come to realize that he does not need to dislike the whole person but can dislike only certain parts of that person. In that way his anger need not be overwhelming to him or others.

Lesson 6. You Should

Choose a partner, preferably someone you "boss around."

Partners take turns playing the following roles with each other.

Role A: "You should . . ." (Keep telling B all he should be and do.)

Role B replies: "You are right. I am so dumb I don't even know how to do that." (B finds many ways to agree with A.)

Change roles.

How did you feel when you were playing Role A? How did you feel playing Role B? Which role did you like better? Are there times when you really play one of those roles? If so, when and with whom? Are there times when you see people around you playing those roles? Who plays them?

When do they play them? How and when might these roles be harmful to you? How and when might these roles be useful?

With primary children, have A be a parent and B a child.

Lesson 7. Let Off Steam

Sit in a circle.

Each one of you is to tell the others in the group what's bothering you. Direct your comments personally. "Laurie, you bug me when you chew your gum and snap it with your mouth open. Robert, I could kick you when you walk by my desk and knock my things off. Irene, you make me mad when you sit next to me and act silly."

Do not defend yourself when others address you. Just listen to what others have to say to you. You will have your turn to let off steam too.

Now, think about the things that were said to you. Sometimes you can change the things about yourself that bother others. Sometimes you cannot. Were some things said to you that you can and are willing to change? If so, state it to the person who said it to you. "I will try not to snap my gum when I am with you. If I forget, let me know before I start to bother you," says Laurie to the one who addressed her.

This is an excellent lesson when you sense that there is a great deal of nondirected bickering and arguing going on in the group. Having the opportunity to get everything out in the open allows the child to air his resentments and to see what demands are being made of him and which of those he can attend to.

Variation

Have a "Mutter Time." Each child in the group sits in a circle and mutters about all the things that are bothering him.

Nothing good can be said about anyone during that time. (Allow ten minutes.)

How do you feel when you are muttering? How do you feel when you know everyone else is muttering too? How do you feel after "Mutter Time" is over? Did you stop muttering?

Lesson 8. Gang Aggression

Divide the class into groups of eight to ten. In dividing the groups try to have aggressive children equally distributed.

Take time with your group to learn to operate as a single unit. Link yourselves together physically in some way. You can hold hands, link arms or fingers, but find some way to be together.

Develop a sound that belongs to your group. You can hum, grunt, moan, do anything you want to make a sound together. Now find a way to move together. Stay away from the other groups. Remain with your group long enough to really move and make a noise as one unit.

Now move out and encounter the other groups in the room staying in your group and making your sound. Be aware of what happens to you and your group.

Move back to your own group's space. Talk about what happened. Do you behave differently when you have the support of the group? How are you different in a group? How are you the same?

Now imagine this group (*indicate one*) has "it." All the other groups want "it." (*"It" is not defined or identified in the game.*) Experiment with how you and your group can get "it."

Allow time for a discussion of what happened with the game before leaving it. Depending on the group, you might explore situations that are real outside the realm of the game. What happens when two children gang up on one? What happens when one gang of people challenges another gang? What happens when one group outnumbers the other group? What feelings do you experience when you're in a big group (classrooms) that you don't feel in a small group (peer group)? When do we engage in ritualistic aggression (competitive games)? What does ritualistic aggression do for us? What happens in some riots? How come the police don't simply shoot all the demonstrators? How come the demonstrators don't shoot all the policemen?

Variation

Indicate that one group has "it" and wants to give "it" to the others. Allow time to experiment with giving "it" to the others.

Is it easier to give or to receive? How do you feel giving, how do you feel receiving?

Lesson 9. Make Me

This is a lesson designed to help clarify the roles of responsibility within a classroom. If you have a drained, heavy feeling after being with the class for just an hour and feel as if you have been trying to push a huge boulder up a steep hill, try playing a game of "Make Me."

Ask, "What do I make you do?" List all the responses from the class on the blackboard so that everyone can see the list. Do not judge the responses or start justifying your behavior. Just receive all they have to say. Once the list is complete, and it may be enormous, sit with and be in the group and just look at the list.

For a while, nothing may seem to be happening. Wait. This is what could happen. One boy, Jeff, begins to chuckle. Others join in. Soon most of the group is laughing and shaking their heads. With such a list in front of them, everyone sees how absurd it is to expect one person to make them do all those things. Jeff then goes to the blackboard, takes the eraser, and says, "I said you make me do this but I can really do it for myself, so I'll take it off." He then erases his own statement and returns to his seat. Another child follows his example. In each case the child says, "I can take this." At the end there are still some things on the board. We then talk together about how we can help the child who still feels there are certain things he or she has to be "made" to do. Each of us then offers what we feel we can realistically do to help out in those situations. One girl leaves her statement "You make me do spelling." One child offers to give her advance notice that it is going to be time to work on spelling so she can be prepared. The boy who sits next to her says he will get the materials needed for both of them, and then continues by saying, "You'll just have to do the rest yourself!"

See if you and your class can invent or create your own game of "Make Me."

Lesson 10. Boys and Girls

All the boys in the class write, "Girls are . . ." and finish that sentence in a few words, with many sentences, or with a paragraph. Do not put any names on the paper.

All the girls in the class write, "Boys are . . ." and finish that sentence in a few words, with many sentences, or with a paragraph. Do not put any names on the paper.

When all are finished, have a boy collect the girls' papers. Have a girl collect the boys' papers. The boy reads aloud all the papers written by boys about girls. The girl reads aloud all the papers written by girls about boys. Allow time for discussion.

Discuss male and female roles. How do we get them? How and when do they create problems? How do they offer solutions? What happens if we try on different roles? What would happen if you played the "wrong" role? How do you decide if a person is playing a "wrong" role?

Lesson 11. A Funny Story

Think of something funny. It can be something you said to someone, something that was said to you, or something funny that you did. It must be something funny that happened to you and not something that happened to someone else. Share your funny story with a friend as if it were happening now.

How many of you shared a story in which someone got hurt? (It could be someone that got hurt physically or got their feelings hurt.)

When do you use humor to hurt someone? When has someone used humor to hurt you? Is it possible to hide a cruel statement in a joke? How? How else do people get hurt with humor? Instead of hiding your anger in humor, how else might you express it?

Be aware of the times you experience humor during the day. Be aware of when you use it to hide anger. Be aware of when others use it to hide their anger.

With advanced children, you might want to discuss various categories of humor, such as farce, satire, slapstick, and irony.

Lesson 12. I Can't at School

Think of something in school you would like to change. State all the reasons you can't change it.

Now restate those sentences beginning with "I won't" instead of "I can't."

How many excuses did you discover? How many real barriers did you discover? (There *are* real barriers. Do not imply or let the child believe that anything can be changed simply by restating the problem.)

Lesson 13. I Can't at Home

Think of something in your life you would like to change. State all the reasons you can't change it.

Now restate those sentences beginning with "I won't" instead of "I can't." Really listen to yourself as you say it this time.

Examples: I would like to make a new blouse. I can't because I don't have time. I can't because I do not have the materials. I can't because my mother won't help me.

Change to: I would like to make a new blouse. I won't because I don't have time. I won't because I do not have the materials. I won't because my mother won't help me.

Do you feel any difference? Which statements were really true statements? Which were merely statements of excuses?

Lesson 14. Frustrating Games

"The Killer" game

Pass out playing cards or numbered slips of paper equal to the number of people in the group. One student is identified as "the Killer" by a specific card (the ace of spades) or slip (number 3), determined beforehand. The Killer kills off people by winking at them. The object is for the Killer to eliminate as many people as possible without being identified. A person who is "killed" must wait a few seconds and then fall over dead. He is then out of the game. If someone who is alive thinks he knows the killer, he can "accuse," but only if he has actually seen him winking at someone. A false accusation eliminates the accuser.

If the group is larger than ten, have more than one game going at a time, have more than one Killer, or have the players mill around. When a player is "killed," he sits down. It adds to the excitement of the game if you play it in a dim light.

> Discuss what happened with the game.
>
> How did you feel when you're the Killer?
>
> How did you feel when you knew a wink could "kill" you?
>
> How did you feel about protecting the identity of the Killer after he killed you?

Black magic

A and B both know the "magic" in "Black Magic."

B leaves the room while A and the rest of the group decide upon an object to be "it."

B returns to the room, and A asks him, "Is it . . . (names a specific object)?" B knows that A will at some time ask about a black object, and the next object named will be "it."

Example: B leaves the room. A and the group choose the teacher's desk to be "it." B is asked to return to the room.

A asks, "Is it the round table?" B replies, "No."

A goes on. "Is it that piece of chalk?" B says, "No."

"Is it the big hand of the clock?" (The big hand of the clock is black.) B replies, "No."

"Is it the teacher's desk?" B replies, "Yes."

When someone else in the group thinks he knows the "magic," he leaves the room. The group again decides upon an item. He comes back to see if he knows the magic. If he has figured out the trick, he will have "Black Magic." If he misses, he rejoins the group and continues to figure out what makes "Black Magic."

How did you feel when you didn't know the magic? How did you feel when you finally discovered it? How did you feel about knowing it and not telling your friends?

Gestalt *game*

Materials: An assortment of pencils.

A and B know how to play the game.

A carefully and elaborately arranges all the pencils into some form. He then says, "Look at the whole thing and tell me the number I am making." B then tells what number it is.

A makes quite a fuss about arranging the pencils "just so." He also subtly but openly indicates the number the arrangement "represents" by placing his fingers on the table or floor so that B can read them. B tells the answer from A's fingers, not from what he has done with the pencils.

When someone in the group figures out what is happening, he calls out the numbers until someone else catches on.

How did you learn the game? How did you feel when you discovered the answer? How did you feel about those who still could not figure it out?

The answers to this game were easy once you knew how to get them. What other things do you know about that are easy once you know how?

The next time you tell someone "it's easy," see if you should add, "once you know how." The next time someone tells you something is easy, see if they are leaving out "once you know how."

UNIT EIGHT
Nature

An important aspect of self-realization is the establishment of identity or unity with nature. Much of man's highest enjoyment is found in his experiences with and appreciation of the beauty of nature. Recently, we have begun to realize that man's irresponsible disregard for nature, his depletion of natural resources, and the obliteration of natural beauty may result in the destruction of most, if not all, life on earth. Man's relations to nature now demands our attention. With the awareness that the natural world is shrinking and may be destroyed, a growing number of people are seeking ways of ensuring its preservation.

Increasing emphasis in education is being placed on developing this awareness and concern. It is recognized that transmission of facts alone will not solve the problems of our environment and ecology. Living in harmony with nature must become a personal value and objective of each individual. A person's educational experiences should enable him to discover or rediscover his place in nature and bring the realization that any separation is probably artificial and possibly destructive.

Unfortunately, it is very difficult to bring an identity with nature into the average classroom setting with any degree of reality. Older schools have been encroached upon by the ever widening cities. Newer schools are made of synthetic materials, on land that has been scraped bare by bulldozers. At both, what landscaping there is has been designed by man. There are few schools designed around natural settings, and in those that are, the settings are usually used in traditional ways: Children learn in the classroom, walk in the halls, play on the blacktop.

In such environments it is difficult for the child to experience nature in any way that matters to him. He has no way to develop values for living in harmony with nature when he lives in an environment that locks it out. However, confluent education, in which discovering one's identity is a primary goal, affords some opportunities for dealing with nature in a real way in the classroom. The child who is engaged in self-assessment must assess his environment as well, and he must receive assessments about himself from others in his environment.

Look for natural environments that are still available. (At the very least, films of nature are available for classroom use.) The children can make terrariums and observe the environment in them. Go on a field trip to a park and encourage the children to experience it in a new way—blindfolded and/or barefoot, or imagining that it is vanishing. How would life be without plants, trees, and parks? Introduce the children to a tree or a patch of grass. Let each child "become" that tree or patch of grass. Let him develop the role as he sees it. Let him move into it in his own way, in as many different ways as possible, dance it, paint it, write a story entitled "I am a tree."

In any environment, urban or rural, and in any section of the country, children can become aware of how they respond to the weather around them. How do you usually feel on windy days? How do you act out those feelings? How do you feel on foggy or rainy days? How do you act out those feelings? How do you experience the colors around you in the morning hours as compared to noontime or dusk? Which time of the day feels best to you? What do you like about it? Give the child many opportunities to talk about nature and his experiences with it. The kinds of questions he asks and the things he discovers on his own can change his experiences from "fun and games" to very meaningful affective-cognitive experiences.

The following lessons provide the child with opportunities

to experience more, do more, discover more. They also de-emphasize words as a way of knowing and stress various parts of the body. These lessons help the child to express and amplify the power that is within him. It is in the vastness of nature that some of this power can be tapped. The child can learn to "tune in," to use his total being as a way of knowing. Many of the lessons require the child to be outdoors so that he can experience more of his environment than the limits of the classroom. To be outdoors provides more contact with nature and natural things and allows the child a oneness with nature that can lead to a more integrated, more aware self.

Be sure to read through these lessons to see how they apply to the particular setting of your school. Some can be done in any school anywhere. Others may have to be adapted. Still others may have to be omitted. See if they can serve to spark your imagination. For example, the children in Santa Barbara, California, would rarely have an opportunity to make trails in the snow for other children to follow. But they could do a similar activity by making trails in the sand at the beach while on a field trip.

Objectives

To be able to identify familiar sounds in the environment through listening.

To be able to utilize characteristics of a day for a learning experience.

To distinguish between man-made and natural changes.

To use listening as a way of knowing.

To be able to use one's entire body as a way of knowing.

Lesson 1. Sound Simile

Discuss the "sounds of nature." Talk about rain, wind, thunder, birds, water, leaves, etc.

Complete the sentence, "When I hear _____,
I think of _____." Use a sound of nature
in the first blank.

Lesson 2. A Sound Walk

Divide a piece of paper in half. On one side write "Man-
Made Sounds," and on the other side write "Natural Sounds."
Go for a walk on the school grounds for about fifteen
minutes. Listen to the sounds around you. As you hear
them, write them on your paper under "Man-Made Sounds"
or "Natural Sounds."

Compare your list with someone else's list. What did both
of you hear? What did you hear that the other one didn't
hear? Were there any sounds that you heard that made it
hard for you to decide which category they belonged in?
If so, what?

The amount of time you allow for the sound walk will
depend on the interest level of the children and the time you
have available. It is important to allow enough time so that
the children will have an opportunity to listen for quiet,
subtle sounds as well as louder ones.

Variation

Gor for a fifteen-minute walk on the school grounds. Come
back to the room and make a list of the sounds you heard.
Go for another fifteen-minute walk. Make a list again, account-
ing for the differences. (Example: I listened more. It was
noisier. I went to different places. I remembered more of
what I heard.)

Lesson 3. A Feeling Walk

Go for a fifteen-minute walk on the school grounds, touching and feeling everything possible along the way.

Talk about the things you felt. What did you like to feel? What didn't you like to feel? What was there about it that you didn't like?

A familiar schoolground is an excellent place to do this. The child is used to seeing all of the items there but will come to "see" them in a very different way while on the feeling walk.

Lesson 4. Total Sense Walk

Go for a walk around a familiar area or somewhere new or special. For three minutes concentrate on the sounds around you. For three minutes be aware of the smells around you. For three minutes touch everything you can in your environment. In the next three minutes see everything around you as if for the first time. Now sit down and close your eyes. Spend the next three minutes on taste. Put something in your mouth—a leaf, a piece of grass. Complete your walk, keeping sense activity in the foreground. Allow yourself to experience whatever presents itself. See if you can let sensations fuse and blend into a total experience.

Don't be concerned with exact timing. If the child spends the entire time on one or two senses, let him be. He can do the others at another time.

Lesson 5. Acting Out Nature

This is a type of "class participation story" described earlier. Choose an occurrence in nature that can be acted out by children. There should be many parts for them to choose from.

The one described here can be used after seeing a movie or reading a book describing seed dispersal. The parts are seeds, animals, wind, sun, water, and soil. Have each child choose a part to play before the story begins.

You are all seeds in a pod. (Just the seeds act out this part.) It is a tight pod. You cannot move. (Add details appropriate to the class needs.)

Next the water comes. (The child who is water comes and waters the pods.) Some pods grow larger. Some do not get enough water, and so do not begin to grow.

The water goes away. The sun comes out to warm the seed pods. The pods break open. The pods are now many seeds.

The wind comes and tumbles and rolls the seeds in all directions.

The animals come and run around in the seeds. Some seeds get stuck in the animals' fur and some of the animals take the seeds for food.

Now all the seeds find a place to settle. Stay there, since seeds cannot move on their own.

The wind blows soil over some of the seeds.

The water comes and washes soil over some of the seeds.

The sun comes out to make the soil warm so that the seeds begin to grow.

The water comes to give the seeds moisture to help them grow into a plant.

The wind comes and gently blows the plant.

Animals run and play in and around the plant.

Soon the plant begins to grow new seed pods. These pods fall to the ground and the whole story begins all over again.

The themes on acting out nature are limited only by your own imagination and ability to transpose written or seen material into stories that can be acted out.

Some other suggested themes:

A storm and its effects on the rivers, animals, homes, and people.

Changes of weather, from sun to rain.

The cycle of a drop of water.

The life cycle of any plant or animal.

A food chain, either in the ocean or on the land.

An advanced class took the basic idea of this lesson and developed a play at the end of a health unit on the digestive system. They had their own narrator. The teacher was just an observer. The class "became" the digestive system, with students taking the various parts of the system. They gave each part a voice and an action, based on their own knowledge and awareness of the part.

Be sure you allow adequate space for these activities. It may be necessary to push all furniture out of the way or go to a multipurpose room or, even better, go outside.

The lesson described above might be followed by these questions:

How did you feel when you were in the seed pod at the beginning? (Let "pods" answer.)

How did the water help the pods? What might happen if too much water falls at one time? What might happen to seeds if there isn't enough rain?

How did the wind help the seeds? Could it be harmful too? How?

What did the animals do with the seed pods? What might happen if the animals didn't take some seeds? (Animals died. Plants died because of lack of space, resources.)

How did you feel when you were a growing plant? Did you like the sun, wind, and water? What did you like about them? What did you not like about them? When did they help? When did they cause harm?

How did you feel about growing more seeds? Why did you grow so many of them? What might happen if you grew only two or three seeds? What would happen to animals who need to eat the seeds? (Let animals answer.)

If you were to do this over again, what part would you like to play?

Although you would not necessarily use all of these questions, it is important to allow the children to express the feelings evoked by playing the various parts. This is also an excellent opportunity for discussing negative feelings and provides experiences in answering "what if" or "what might happen" questions.

Lesson 6. Changes

Set out at least three items that will begin to change. Examples: A dish containing metal objects and water. A pot of dirt with seeds buried in it. A goldfish in a bowl. A dish containing an egg with no shell.

Look at each of these items. What do you see? Draw or write a description of each one. Compare your description with someone else's to be sure you did not leave anything out.

(Wait three days.) Look carefully at each item again. What do you see? Compare what you see now with what you saw three days ago. What things have changed? Are there other things in our room that have changed in the last three days? What other changes do you know about that have occurred in the last three days?

Which items seem not to have changed at all? What in our room is the same today as it was three days ago? What other things do you know that have stayed the same over the last three days?

When do you like things to change quickly? How do you think you would feel if every day everything were changed in this room? What if you had different places to sit, different books to read, a different teacher, different children to be with you?

When do you like things to change slowly? How do you think you would feel if nothing ever changed in here? What if you had the same places to sit all the time, the same books all the time, the same teacher all the time, the same children with you all the time?

Be aware of the changes around you during the day. Be aware of the times you feel there is too much change, occurring too quickly, and the times you feel there is not enough change, or it's occurring too slowly to satisfy you.

Variation

If possible, bring a picture of your school that was taken some years ago.

Discuss all the changes around the school since the picture was taken. Visit some place that has changed. For example, walk through a tract of homes where an orchard once stood. Look for remains of the orchard.

Imagine changes around the school that will occur in the future. What might a picture of the school look like if it were taken twenty years from now?

Lesson 7. Natural Collage

Go for a walk around the school and find one natural thing that in some way symbolizes you. You might choose a rock to symbolize your strength. You might choose a leaf to symbolize your love of being with a large group of people. You might choose a weed to symbolize your rebellious self. Let your imagination go. Look at many things. Try them on. How does a rock fit me? What part of me fits a rock?

You can choose the same item as someone else, for entirely different reasons.

Bring the item that fits you best back to the classroom. Each one in the class is to put his item into a collage. Discover where you want to put your item in relation to the total collage, in relation to where others have put their items. Experiment with several different placements before leaving it there.

Now talk about yourself as your item in relation to where you are in the collage. Talk in the present tense and use "I." Example: "I am an orange flower. I am soft and tender. I am on the very edge of the collage. I am there so I will not get bruised or broken by the rocks and sticks." "I am a weed. I am long and rangy. I am in the center of the collage. I will eventually spread out and completely cover the collage."

Lesson 8. Rainy-Day Activities

Take any day that has an accentuated weather feature and look for some way to take advantage of it. Usually teachers face rainy, hot, or windy days with something akin to dread. See if there is something special you can do with the children because of the weather. Here are some starters.

Sprinkle different colors of powered tempera on a piece of paper. Place it in the rain where it can be observed. Watch the rain paint a picture. Bring it in when you feel it is finished.

Concentrate on the sound of rain for a set period of time. Graph it, draw it, dance it.

Read "Chapter IX, in which Piglet is entirely surrounded by water," from *Winnie the Pooh,* by A. A. Milne.

Place a stick upright in a puddle. Observe it several times during the day. Watch the water rise or fall.

Watch a puddle grow. Measure around it with a piece of string. Measure it every fifteen minutes. Compare the length of string each time. (Each time a different child bundles up and "braves the storm" in order to measure it.)

When the rain stops, but while water is still running, have a contest floating paper boats down street gutters, rain drains, free-form ditches. Time the paper boats. Measure the distance they travel. Compute the speed at which they travel.

Watch raindrops sliding down the windowpanes. Time them with a stopwatch. Graph them. Imagine you are a raindrop. Write a story about your journey. Begin with "I am a raindrop."

Learn to read weather maps. Where else is it raining? What might the children be doing there?

Learn to read rain tables. Make your own and keep it up to date. Compare it with last year's data (available in local newspapers in your nearby library). Make predictions for next year.

Write words that describe the sound of rain. Write words that describe how you feel about rain. Use as many of those words as possible to make a poem or story about rain.

Work in groups to make a list of things that go up in the rain (e.g., rivers, umbrellas, earthworms, etc.). Be as creative as possible. Explain your list to another group.

Work in groups to make a list of things that go down in the rain (hairdos, flags, hillsides, etc.). Be as creative as possible. Explain your list to another group.

Lesson 9. Snowy-Day Activities

Go outside and catch a snowflake in your mouth, on your eyelid, on your elbow, on your knee. Talk about how it felt to you and what happened to it.

When it is not snowing, but snow is on the ground, one

child is to go out and make a snow trail. Another child is to find the trail and go on it. Pretend you are the person who made the trail. How do you feel when walking in his footsteps? What might it be like to be him?

Make snowmen, snow women, and snow sculptures.

Have a relay race getting dressed and undressed in snow togs from head to foot.

Imagine you get snowed in here at school. What then? Where could you sleep? What could you eat? How would you manage? What would you like about getting snowed in? What wouldn't you like?

Go for a walk in the snow. If a park or a woods is nearby look for animal tracks and other signs of life. In a city, observe traffic patterns in the now. What patterns do cars make? What patterns do people make? Can you see other kinds of patterns in the snow? What do you imagine from what you see?

Go sledding. Use inner tubes, plastic disks, sleds. Measure distance, compare results.

Choose a certain thing, tree, a fence, or a building, that you can observe from the classroom. Record, in pictures or writing, how it responds to the snow, how it changes in appearance.

Build a snow fort. Engage another class in a snowball fight.

Lesson 10. Cold-Day Activities

Put out a pan of water and see if it will freeze. How long will it take? Make predictions. Who came closest?

Be aware of feeling cold on various parts of your body. How do your hands feel cold? How do your feet feel cold? Your nose? Your cheeks? How do they feel when they change from cold to warm?

How do you feel when you are bundled up for the cold?

How do you move? What don't you like about being bundled up? What do you like?

Bake bread in the class. Watch the changes, enjoy the smells, savor the taste. (You can make it from scratch, or bring in frozen dough ready to defrost, rise, and bake.)

Draw pictures on frosty windows. Watch them change.

Discuss "How cold is cold?" Look at temperatures in other places, particularly cold places. Would someone at the North Pole think our temperature is cold?

Go outside and send smoke signals to one another with your breath. Did you send a message? Did you receive a message? How well can you communicate with smoke signals?

Pop popcorn. Eat it while it's hot.

Make sugar cookies in the shape of your initials.

Make a class stew. Everyone bring something to make the stew.

Lesson 11. Hot-Day Activities

Bob for apples. Feel the cool water on your face, in your hair. Do not wipe the water off, but let it evaporate. Be aware of your face and how it feels.

Go out in the sun and engage in a vigorous activity. Play a game, have a relay race, or run a lap. Come into the classroom. Turn off the lights. Sit or lie down. Read a story, listen to a record, or play a quiet game. Be aware of your body as it adjusts to a cooler temperature and a quiet activity.

Record the temperature every thirty minutes. Write one word that describes how you feel at that temperature. Make a graph to show the temperatures. Make a graph to show your feelings.

Think "cool." Go to the coolest place in your body and work from there. See if it makes a difference in the temperature of the room.

Work out the details for a class swim in a public or private pool. How will we get there, what will we need to take, what time will we leave and return? Do it.

Have a water-balloon throwing contest. Choose a partner. How far away from each other can you stand and still toss the balloon back and forth?

Observe changes of color of your skin in the sun. Wrap a piece of adhesive tape around a finger. Leave it there for one week. When you take it off, compare the difference.

Go swing. Feel the heat when you work. Feel the air as it passes over and around you.

Lesson 12. Windy-Day Activities

Go to an open space with a crepe-paper streamer. Let the wind take the streamer. Measure how far your streamer went with the wind. Whose goes the farthest?

Crumple a piece of paper. Throw it into the wind. Follow it around. Move when it moves, move where it moves.

Listen to the sounds of the wind in the room. What sounds are strange because of the wind? How does your home sound in the wind? What do windy sounds remind you of?

Run into the wind. Run away from the wind. Feel the difference. Time a run into the wind. Time a run away from the wind. Compare the difference.

Make pinwheels. Pin them to your pencil. Go into the wind. Which directions does the wind come from? Feel the wind push the pinwheel, the pencil, and your hand. Talk about the way man uses the wind with windmills.

Make kites. Go fly them.

Lie on the ground. Feel the wind on your body. Stand up. Feel the wind now. Now build or find a shelter from the wind.

Lie on your back and watch the wind move the clouds. Find as many different things as you can in the clouds.

UNIT NINE
Space

One way to experiment with and develop confluent education is to choose something old and familiar and look at it in a new way in order to derive new meanings in terms of its effects on us.

To do this in a classroom setting, look at the "space" in and around a classroom. In every way we deal with that space, we should be able to derive new meanings in terms of boundaries and territories, rules and regulations, and how interpersonal relationships are affected by space.

Imagine entering a classroom. How is that space used? How does that use reflect the life that is being experienced in the classroom? What pleasurable sights do we see? In what way does the use of space in this room reflect life for the child as we would like to see it? How does the space include the child? What signs of his life do we see? Is the space organized so that the child can move about in it on his own, or do his actions have to be dependent on an adult? What is unpleasant? In what way does the use of space seem to make life more difficult for the child, less rewarding than it might be? Is this the child's room, or is he just a visitor here? Is he in control of this room, or is he controlled by the room?

Now imagine experimenting with making some changes in that classroom. The easiest changes to make are those of organization. Imagine that we have seen some ways in which the organization of materials does not allow the child to use them to his advantage: Perhaps the art materials are too far away from the working area, the arrangement of the science materials discourages the child from taking them out and experimenting with them, the area for noisy activities is too close to the area for quiet activities. Even a simple organizational change can have multiple effects. When art and science materials are easily available, the child demands time to be able to use them. A child engrossed in a science investigation he has set up resents leaving it to join the group for a teacher-directed activity. A change in organization may necessitate some time-schedule changes as well as the formulation of new rules and regulations for how and when equipment can be used. It may also require a teacher to abandon his plans and go with what the child develops as a plan for using his space, at least for certain time periods.

Developing an awareness of the space of the classroom can bring out conflicts over the use of space and the use of things in that space. These conflicts are present in every classroom, but they are not usually dealt with directly. When there is space for only one child and three children want it, what happens? Who makes the decision? How is it decided who will get the space? By playing that out in a lesson, the children become aware of the many times they are faced with decisions on how they use their space and the many ways it must be shared.

Conflict between group and individual needs for space must also be explored. The child involved in a group activity has to share the available space, and still he is aware of his own need for space. New boundaries may have to be established. Sometimes it is possible to change boundaries, to expand the available space by moving to another place or going outside. Sometimes it is necessary to learn ways to live with that conflict.

At first, even simple changes in the use of space may seem to have overwhelming effects for the teacher. Many decisions may have to be made on the basis of the effects of the change —rearranging time schedules, making new rules and regulations, deciding how and when space can be used in new ways. But gradually the child can make these decisions as he begins to have an awareness of himself in his space. He experiments with ways to share his space with others. He becomes aware of how his space is influenced by the things and people in his space. He becomes aware of how he invades the space of others in physical ways—and in other ways too, as when another child reprimands him for having disturbed his "imaginary space" by talking out loud in a fantasy game. He begins to experiment on his own with making changes in the space of the room and watching how that change affects the group. Others express how his changes affect them. He learns to express his feelings about how the changes others make affect him. He experiments with changing rules and regulations, and so learns to appreciate those that aid him and others in sharing and using a space. He learns to accept rules made by others with greater understanding. Gradually, he gains control of the use of his space and further develops his responsibility.

These lessons begin with the teacher looking at his classroom. You are asked to look at the space of your classroom in a new way. Then the child is asked to focus on his space in the room. From there, other children are introduced to his space. Finally, we look at the space beyond the classroom, at home and in the school. Each lesson is concerned with helping the child to be aware of his space, both how he affects it and how it affects him.

Objectives

To be able to observe the physical space available.

To be able to share the available space with others in the group.

To experiment with making changes in a space.

To be able to verbalize the effects of changes on yourself and others in the group.

To be able to verbalize how other people and things influence the rules and regulations for the use of space.

Lesson 1. Teacher's Room

Walk into your room. Imagine that you are a foreign visitor, here to observe and to learn about the teacher and students who live in that room. Here are some questions that might help you to "see." How is the room organized? How do you think that organization aids or hinders learning activities? How much "child space" can you observe? How do you know it is "child space"? How much space is shared? How do you know?

Observe the children using the space of the classroom. What invisible boundaries do they observe? What signs do you see that tell you a child lives in the room? What signs do you see that tell you an adult lives in the room? Who put the furniture in its current arrangement? How do you know? Is there a dominant feature in the room? Who is responsible for its being there?

If you were a child entering the room, would you feel it belonged to you or to the teacher? How do you know?

If you were the child, what would you like about the room? What wouldn't you like?

These questions do not have correct responses. They are asked in order to help you become aware of the space of your room and how it is being used. How it is being used necessarily reflects what living and learning occur there.

Lesson 2. My Space

Sit in your normal place in the room. Close your eyes. Take a few deep breaths. Relax. Listen to the sounds around you. Listen to the sounds going on inside of you.

Slowly, slowly reach out with your hands and explore the space in front of you. Reach up and explore the space over your head. Explore the space behind you. Reach down and explore the space underneath you. Explore the space all around you, even the child sitting next to you if he is in your space. Now use your feet and legs to explore some more space around you. Slowly open your eyes.

The space around you can be defined as "your space." It is the space you are in, the amount of space you are taking up at any given time.

Where is there a lot of space around you? (Above their heads.) Where is there very little space for you? When you had your eyes closed, which spaces seemed to go on and on? Which spaces seemed very small? How much space do you usually like to have around you? When can you have that amount of space in this room? When do you have a smaller space than you like to have? What do you do then? Are there times when you have a larger space than you like to have? What do you do then? As you go through the day, be aware of the different amounts of space you have available for your use. Be aware of when you wish you had more space, when you wish you had less space, and when the space feels just right.

Lesson 3. More Space

Walk around the space of our room. Imagine it is the very first time you have been here. Take your time as you walk around. Touch, smell, taste, listen to as much as possible.

Now find a space you experience as a public space—a space that is open and shared by everyone. Find a space you experience as a private space—a space that is closed and for you only. Find a space just big enough for you. Find a space big enough for everyone. Join everyone in that space. Talk about what you discovered about the different spaces you visited.

Do not be concerned with exact definitions of terms in this lesson. Let the child show you how he experiences different spaces. For example, the child might experience closed space as a small physical space, such as a cupboard, or he might experience it as pulling himself into a tight ball and closing his eyes out in the middle of the room. If a term seems to confuse him, or if he does not know how to respond, let him experiment with developing a definition.

Lesson 4. Physical Space

Stand in a space of your own so that you are not touching anyone and you have enough room to move about somewhat without touching anyone.

Imagine that you are beginning to grow larger. Use your arms, your feet, your neck, your entire body to take up more space. Stand on tiptoes, stretch your back, hold your head as high as possible. Take up as much space with your body as you possibly can.

Now slowly, slowly, begin to shrink and shrivel. Become as small as you possibly can. Tuck all of yourself into a small ball. Become smaller, smaller. Take up as little space with your body as you possibly can.

Slowly begin to unfold yourself and stretch again. Do it in slow motion. Feel your body stretch and expand. See if you can become bigger this time than you were last time. Take more space.

Shrink again, very slowly. Make yourself as small as possible again. Do it in slow motion. Feel how you make yourself take up less space.

Now unfold, and take up your usual amount of space. How did you feel when you stretched as large as possible? How did you feel when you were as small as possible? When is it possible for you to stretch out and take a lot of space in our room? (Perhaps when using puzzles or Cuisenaire rods, or playing games.) How do you feel when you take up a lot of space? Are there times when you have to make yourself as small as possible in our room? (Perhaps when lining up, sitting with the entire group, crowding to be able to see something.) How do you feel then? What other places do you know about that allow you to stretch out and take a lot of space? (On the playground, at home.) What other places do you know about that require you to take as little space as possible?

Lesson 5. A Tight Space

Sit on the floor by yourself. Close your eyes. Imagine that you are sitting inside a big cardboard box. Feel the cardboard underneath you. See the four sides of the box all around you.

Now shut the lid of the box, with you inside. Imagine the box is getting smaller and smaller. Pull yourself closer together or else the box will push against you. Don't push the lid up. Don't move, you're pushing the lid up! Make yourself even smaller, as small as possible. Feel how it is in that tiny box. It is getting hot and stuffy in there. Hotter and hotter. As it gets hotter and hotter, you feel you must have air, but you are going to have to push your way out of your box. The box wants to hold you in, but you must get out so you can breathe. Push the box. Come out!!

Take a deep breath. Feel the air as it goes through your nose, and into your lungs. Feel the hot, used air as it leaves your body.

Are there times in our classroom when you feel as if

you are in a tight, stuffy place? (Sometimes when coming in from the playground, sometimes when taking a test or working on something difficult, sometimes when everything is closed to show a movie.)

Are there times whon you get into tight spaces in other places? (Riding a crowded bus, being in an elevator, sharing any small place with many people.)

How does your body respond to tight spaces? What do you usually do when you get into a tight space? What happens to you when you cannot get out of a tight space as soon as you want to? How do you feel when you finally get out?

Remember, a tight space can be psychological as well as physical.

Lesson 6. 100 Inches of String

Measure out a piece of string 100 inches long. Use that string to mark the boundaries of a space. Put yourself into the space of your 100 inches. How well do you fit in there? See how many different kinds of spaces you can make with your 100 inches of string. Make a small space with it. Make as large a space as you can. Make a space with wavy boundaries. Make a space with straight boundaries.

Go outside and find spaces that will fit into your 100 inches of string. Can you put a tree into your string? How would you do that? (Wrap the string around the base of the tree.) Can you put a bicycle into your string? Can you put a chair into your string? Experiment with your string on your own.

Talk about what could and could not be encompassed with the 100 inches of string.

Now put your string around a space you like. Write about the things in your space.

How did you feel about the spaces you could make? If you were to do this again, what would you do over again? What would you change?

Lesson 7. A Full Box

Bring a large cardboard box into the room.

Look at the box. How many books do you imagine we could put in the box? How many desks do you imagine would fit in there? How many of you would fit into that box?

One of you get into the box. Do you have enough room for yourself in there? Do you have room for someone else? If so, choose someone to join you.

Continue adding one child at a time until the children state the box is full.

But here is another child. (Choose one.) He too wants to be in the box. He has nowhere else to be. Somehow all of you in the box will just have to find room for him, even though you have already said the box was full.

Allow the children time to make room for the new child.

How did you make room for one more child in the full box? (Possible solutions: Each child takes up even less space than before, they stretch the boundaries of the box by pushing the sides out, they find a new arrangement of their bodies in order to allow for one more.)

How is the full box like other things you know about? (Making room for a new child in a home that already seems full, making room in a home for company, density of population and overpopulation concerns.)

Lesson 8. Sharing Space

Walk around the room and find the space you like best. Take your time. Experiment with several spaces. When you have made your choice, sit down and experience how it feels to be there. What thoughts come to your mind while you sit there? Do not think about anything, just let thoughts come to you. Look around you. Where are you in relation to other people in the class? Is that important? If so, how?

Now that you have been in your own space for a few minutes, find four other people to join, and together choose a common meeting space, a space that all of you agree is comfortable. Talk to each other and share ideas on your favorite spaces, both inside and outside the classroom. Talk about how you share your favorite spaces at home and other places out of the classroom, and with whom you like to share them.

Lesson 9. Dividing Space

Divide the class into groups. Give each group a large sheet of butcher paper.

Imagine this piece of paper is all the space your group has available. Work together to find a way for each person in your group to share that space. You can divide it up or share it any way you want, but you have to come to a group decision on how to use it.

Allow them time to work to some conclusion.

Different groups of children may solve this in various ways. Some may quickly divide the paper into equal parts, measuring out one share per person. Others may take into account the size of the individuals as a way of dividing the space, giving a large share to a large person and a small share to a small person. Others may not divide it all but may leave all of its available for each to use, as needs for space occur. Encourage multiple and diverse solutions. There is no "right" solution.

Discuss how their solutions are similar to or different from the way space at school is shared. Are there unassigned spaces that are shared according to need (e.g., multipurpose room, gymnasium, library)? Which spaces are of equal size and measured out one-to-one (classrooms, lockers, desks)? Are there some spaces that are assigned according to the size of the children who use them? Do the "big kids" have a greater or lesser share of the playground? Are there bigger classrooms for bigger children?

Lesson 10. Room for One

Place one chair in the middle of the room.
Choose four children to "want" the chair.

Each one of you tell us why you want the chair, what you intend to use it for, why you and not any of the others should have it.

We will listen to your presentations, and then decide who will get the chair.

Discuss: How did you decide who should get the chair? Did you listen to what they said, or did you base your opinion on something else? If so, what else (e.g., "body English," friendship)? How did you feel about denying the others the chair?

(*To the one who got the chair:*) How did you feel about getting the chair, knowing that three others could not have it? Do you feel you had the best reasons for getting it, or did you get it because of something else? If so, what?

(To the other three:) How do you feel about not getting the chair? What do you feel allowed —— to get it? If your were to do this again, what would you do differently? How is this like other things you know about?

Variations

Allow the children opportunities to role-play some of the ideas they suggest at the end of the lesson. Other situations for role-playing follow:

There is one ball available. Four children want to take it out to recess. Who will get it? How will it be decided?

There is one piece of cake left at home. Everyone in the family wants it. Who will get it? How will it be decided?

Six hundred children want to use the playground. How can it be shared? Who will decide? How?

Everyone living in the city demands to be able to use the city in his own way. Who uses what? How is it decided?

Lesson 11. Space Invaders

How do people invade your space? How do other children in this class invade your space?

The children should have many examples of times when they were all set to do something, and another child upset their plans and their space.

When do you usually resent others invading your space?
When is it usually all right for others to invade your space? (When I am bored in my space, when I really don't want it anyway, etc.)

When do you invade the space of others? How do you know you have invaded their space? How do you know if you are welcome in that space? How do you know if you are not welcome?

What things besides people invade your space?

Do bells invade your space? How? When?

Do telephones invade your space? How? When?

Does television ever invade your space? How? When?

For one day, keep a list of people and things that invade your space. Put an X by the ones that pleased you, and an O by the ones that irritated you.

Compare your list with someone else's.

Lesson 12. Making Changes

Find something you want to change in this room. Change it. (Move your desk, rearrange something, change a bulletin board.)

What effect does that change have on others here? How does it affect the space of the room? How does affecting the space affect activities?

Find something you want to change in this room but cannot change by yourself (e.g., new seating arrangements for all, change in schedule). Find someone to help you change it.

What effect does that change have on others here? How does that change affect the space of the room? How does it affect the activities?

Let's live with your changes for a while. Let's see how they work out. If at any time you want to change it back to the way it was, or change it again, do so. Tell someone what made you want to change it again.

Let the children have many opportunities to experiment with making changes in the room. Let them live with some of their "bad choices," as long as they are not harmful to them or others in the room. Let each child decide if his changes help him, hinder him, or are simply made for the sake of change. Let him experiment with as much change as possible, for the only certain thing in his future is that he will be faced with making many changes. In order for him to make responsible changes, he will need to know what effect those changes have on him and his space as well as the effect those changes will have on others and their space.

Variation

Discuss in realistic terms:

Things I can and cannot change by myself.

Things in our class we can and cannot change.

Things our class can and cannot change at school.

Help the child realize what is involved in making changes and the difference between working to make change happen and wishing it would happen.

Lesson 13. Rules for Using Space

Have the children play a regular game of basketball or some other game that has defined boundaries.

Have them play the game again, only this time change the dimensions to a very small space. This can be done either by making the space long and narrow, using the entire length of the court and having it only 6 feet wide, or by confining the game to a small rectangle around one basket.

Play the game again, but this time change the dimensions to a space approximately twice the regular area.

Have the children talk about what happened in the three spaces.

How is the game affected by the amount of space you had available? Which rules of the game made sense when we changed the space? Which ones would you want to change if you were always going to change the space? Which way did you like to play the game the best? (Primary children might prefer the smaller space.) What did you like about playing it that way? What other games do you know about that have space requirements or are played in a specific space? What might happen to each game if you played it in a different amount of space? What new rules might you need to play with a new space?

In what other ways does available space determine its use and its rules? (Compare a four-lane highway to a two-lane road, sharing a bedroom with one child as compared to sharing a classroom with thirty, rules on the playground with rules for using hallways, etc.)

Lesson 14. X Marks the Spot

Make a map of our room. Put an X in the middle of the room. Put an X where you are right now. Put your name by it. Put an X where your best friend is. Put his name by it. Put X's where two more friends are. Put their names by them. If there is some other place in the room where you would rather be, put an X there and circle it.

Now read your map. Make at least three statements based on that information. Share your map and statements with a friend. See if your friend can add another statement to your list based on the information on your map.

You can use this lesson with one on mapping skills. Help a primary child draw the room in relation to north, south, east, and west, placing at least one feature in each direction (e.g., the windows on the north wall, the door on the south wall, etc.). An advanced child might be able to draw the room and everything in it to scale. With either class, once the mapping of the room is complete, let the child place his X's on his own. Don't be concerned if he doesn't put them exactly where they belong. Accurate mapping is not important at this point of the lesson. What is important is that the child have some visual representation of where he sees himself in relation to the space of the room.

Lesson 15. Space at Home

Draw a map of your house. Mark the spaces you use the most at home. Mark the spaces you use the least. Use different colors to define the different spaces.

Do you have a very special, favorite space at home? Mark that space with an X. Describe it. What do you usually do when you are there? How do you usually feel when you are in that space?

Do other people in your home have favorite spaces? Mark those spaces with an O on your map. Describe someone else's favorite space. How do they usually act and what do they usually do when they are in their favorite space?

What spaces in your home are shared spaces? How does your family share the space of your home?

Listen to their answers, and choose a few to extend into role-playing.

Role-play sharing space in the kitchen.

How is that different from the way we share the space where we eat at school? How is it the same?

Role-play sharing space in the living room. Have company come. How does sharing space change when company comes? How is sharing living room space like sharing our room? How is it different? What happens in our room when visitors come?

What might our homes look like if we did not share spaces with each other at home? Draw a home for a family like yours, with each person having the most possible private space, and the least possible shared space. Write a story about what it might be like to live in that kind of house.

Lesson 16. School Space

Imagine that you do not know about your school and how it is used. Imagine that the entire scene is strange and foreign to you. Let's go outside and look at the space of the school. We will walk the geographic boundaries of our school and look into it. From what you see, imagine multiple uses of the spaces you find. What could be done in the grassy areas? In planted areas? Are there walls that could be utilized? How? Are there blacktop areas with and without lines? What could be done with them? What equipment do you see? How might it be used? Are there fences? What could be their purpose or function? Do you see any spaces you have not seen before? How might they be used? Is there a space that is unique to our school (e.g., a hill, gravel area, grove of trees, dirt area)? How could it be used?

Make a map of this school. Mark "child only" spaces on your map. Mark "adult only" spaces. (If there are spaces the children can use only with an adult in attendance, mark it as "adult only" space.) Mark "shared" space, space the children and adults use with equal freedom. Use a different color crayon to mark each kind of space.

Read your map. What does it tell you about space at this school? How do you feel about the use of space at this school? What would you like to see changed? What would you like to see remain the same?

Do only the first paragraph of this lesson with primary and intermediate children. Older, advanced children can go on to the second paragraph if appropriate. Every teacher should do the whole lesson.

UNIT TEN
Art

The idea that the child can create something in art is not new. What confluent education has to offer that *is* new is the idea that the child himself is already a work of art. By isolating certain parts of his body and reproducing them in classic artistic form, in a painting or a print, the child will gain not only an appreciation for art but also a new appreciation of himself and the beauty that is already and always with him.

None of the following art lessons can exist without the child. Each one demands something from him. Each one is offered with the intention of creating continuing experiences in self-discovery, self-appreciation, self-awareness.

In most schools a portion of the child's time is spent in art, dance, drama, or music classes. Unfortunately, however, these classes most often are intended to serve only cathartic functions and therefore remain set off in the child's mind from his heavier academic duties—his "real" lessons. Not so here. These art lessons continue to deal with the feelings and concerns of the child. They are not truly concerned with art in the sense of "works of art." They are concerned with multiple ways to allow the child to express himself. They provide another way for him to work, discover, imagine, and create a continuing awareness of himself.

Like the other units presented so far, the lessons here have the child as the main focus. He is introduced to ways of viewing himself as an object of art, as a collection of objects of art.

A most familiar thing to a child is his name, so that is where we start. The child is then literally taken from head to toe—from an art project dealing with his head to another one dealing with his feet—finding ways to represent himself through art. If a class shows a need for more work dealing with body awareness, the lessons here will show the teacher how various parts of the body can be the central point of an art lesson so that he can provide the class with experiences using other body parts. For example, do "Footprinting" (p. 186), then make hand prints, knee prints, and elbow prints, then draw a picture with your toes holding a crayon, then paint a picture holding a brush in your mouth. Above all, experience yourself as you do so.

From self-awareness we move the child into his environment to explore ways of relating to it in an artistic form. There are lessons in and out of the classroom—helping to reinforce the child's awareness of his environment and his place in nature and blending it with ways that allow him to express his experiences nonverbally, in an artistic form. Again, the particular needs of any given group should dictate how much these lessons are expanded and developed. A class could go beyond the lessons contained here to experience a tree—its leaves, bark, shade, its shelter for birds, its place in ecology, its aesthetic contribution to man—before setting out to express it in artistic form. The objects in a still life can be brought to the child's awareness in the same way. Experience all the qualities of the objects—smell the flowers, taste the fruit, listen to the musical instruments—then express them in an artistic form.

Finally we introduce another person into the artistic scene. These lessons reinforce the child's relationships with those who are around him. Once again, nonverbal communication is stressed. The essential part of these lessons is what the child experiences, not what he produces out of his experiences. He should never have to justify or explain his work. It is important that the teacher and the other children respond to the experience with the child, not to the artistic representation done by the child.

In all these lessons, the main concern is that they be pleasurable experiences for the child. Give him the necessary materials, a basic idea, and let him go. Often what he will do under these circumstances will be very different from any preconceived idea —and much better, both as an "art object" and as a learning experience for him.

Objectives

To represent various body parts in artistic form.
To reproduce a quality of a familar object artistically.
To interpret familiar words artistically.
To interpret something in nature artistically.
To be able to work with another person to produce an artistic form.
To do what one can artistically without self-consciousness.

Lesson 1. My Name

Materials: Graph paper, colored crayons, construction paper, scissors, paste.

Print your name on graph paper in large letters, about three inches high. Trace over your name with a dark crayon. Then outline it with another color. Do this over and over until the letters of your name are full and fat. You might even build them up so that they overlap. Use a variety of colors.

Cut out the shape of your name and mount it on a piece of bright-colored construction paper.

How do you feel about your name now?

Did you discover anything new about your name?

Is there something you particularly don't like about it?

Is there something you particularly like about it?

With primary children, you might have to do the first printing of their names for them. With advanced children, have them do the same thing with words more suited to their interests or concerns: Love, Peace, War, Sex, Hate, etc.

Variation

Fold a sheet of construction paper in half lengthwise. Write your name on the fold. Draw around the letters of your name, making them about ¼" wide. Cut your name out without disturbing the fold. Cut out the spaces inside any loops, such as in l's, a's, o's, etc. Mount your cut-out name onto a contrasting piece of construction paper.

Talk about the design of your name. What does it remind you of? If you were to do this again, how would you write your name differently?

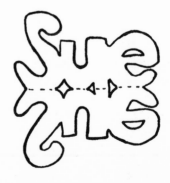

This lesson can be done with names in manuscript print too. Just be sure to keep the fold uncut and make the letters wide enough to touch each other.

Lesson 2. Thumbprint Paintings

Materials: Stamp pads, white construction paper, fine-line felt-tip pens.

Press your thumb onto the stamp pad and then make a print on white construction paper. Repeat until your paper has many thumb prints scattered over it. Now add fine lines to your thumb prints to turn them into drawings, for example, flowers, animals, machines, faces.
What did you discover about your thumb?
What else could you do with your thumb?
How could we do thumb prints again in a different way?
What other body parts might you use?

Advanced children can do this on a large sheet of lightweight paper (colored newsprint) and use it for wrapping paper, or on heavy brown paper (paper bag) before turning it into a book cover.

Lesson 3. What's on My Mind?

Materials: Construction paper, crayons, magazines, paste, scissors.

Draw a silhouette of a head in profile on a piece of construction paper. Make it large. Cut it out. While **doing this,** talk about what's on your mind. What are you thinking about? What thoughts run through your head?

Now paste the profile on a piece of construction paper. Fill the profile with the things that are on your mind. You can cut out pictures from magazines, or you can draw your own pictures.

What did you discover about your mind?

How do you decide what's on your mind?

What was easy or difficult about that lesson?

Variations

Draw a line across the top part of the profile. Put drawings or cut-outs above the line. Draw in your face below the line.

Have a child stand with his profile in the beam of a flashlight while another child traces the outline of his profile onto the construction paper and then proceed as in the lesson.

Lesson 4. Footprinting

Materials: Large sheets of butcher paper, pan of tempera paints, washcloths.

Remove your shoes and socks. Step into a pan of tempera paint and then onto a piece of paper, making footprints all over it. Use different parts of your feet. Tiptoe for a while. Walk on your heels, walk on the sides of your feet. When you are through making your footprint, wipe the paint off your feet with a washcloth before putting your shoes and socks back on.

What can you do with your footprints now? Here are some ideas.

When the paintings are dry, create a story to go with it.

Cut up your footprints and rearrange them into paintings.

Take two types of footprints, a tiptoe and a full foot, cut them out, paste them onto separate sheets of paper, and make up sayings to go under them.

Cut out a footprint and use crayons or pens to make it into something else.

What else can you think of to do with your feet?

What might the picture be like if we each had three feet?

Caution: This is a messy lesson. Cleaning twenty-eight pairs of feet can be a lesson in itself!

Variation

Materials: Recordings of music that has a variety of tempos, themes, and rhythms (Walt Disney's *Fantasia* is excellent for this lesson), pans of tempera paints, large sheets of paper, washcloths.

Listen to the record. Be aware of what you are feeling as you listen to the music.

What movements would you make to go with the music?

What color would you use to go with your feelings and the music?

Step into a color that best shows how you feel.

Step onto your paper and move the way the music makes you want to move. Dance a painting.

Lesson 5. Body Outlines

Materials: Pencils, large sheets of butcher paper, scissors, paints, crayons.

Choose a partner. One of you lie down on your piece of paper. Your partner will trace around your outline, being careful to get the fingers, neck, hair, and shoes on the paper. Then you do the same for your partner.

Cut out your outline. Now fill it in with details. Paint the clothing to match the clothing you are wearing now. Now you have a paper doll of yourself.

Tell a friend something new about you.

How does your paper doll of yourself make you feel?

What would you like to do with your paper doll? If possible, do it. (Hang it up on the wall. Put it in your chair.)

If the child holds his pencil straight up and down and keeps it gently touching his partner, he will get an accurate outline. Allow the children to make corrections before cutting out their outlines if necessary.

Lesson 6. Castles in the Air

This is excellent "warm-up" activity as well as a good way to deal with the statement "I can't draw."

Stand so that there is some room around you. Use your finger as if it were a magic pencil, and use the space around you as a drawing board.

Now let's all draw an imaginary castle. Begin at the bottom and draw the base of your castle. (Stoop down and begin to draw.) Draw your castle as you see it. Is the base made of large stones or small ones? Is it rough or smooth? What color are you painting with?

When you have the base finished, draw the doorway. What is your castle doorway like? What else does your castle need?

As you work drawing your own castle, ask the children questions about what they are doing. Encourage their own ideas and contributions to the game. Stimulate their imaginations. Get them to move their entire body while drawing. Try to get them to take over the conversation, while you continue to be busy on your own castle, following the leads and ideas suggested by the children.

Variation

You can encourage the children to draw anything with this technique. In springtime you may hear, "I can't draw a rabbit. Will you do it for me?" This is a good time to draw rabbits in the air. You may not improve the child's drawing ability with this activity, but you will help him to use the skill he does have unselfconsciously.

Lesson 7. Animated Words

Think of an action word. Write the word, drawing the letters to look like what the word does.

Think of a word that describes how something feels. Write the word, drawing the letters to show how the word feels.

Think of a word that describes an emotion. Write the word, drawing the letters and adding lines in a way that expresses that emotion.

Lesson 8. Familiar Objects

Find a small object to hold. Look at it from every angle. See it as if you were seeing it for the first time. Throw it into the air and catch it. Roll it on the floor. Close your eyes and feel your object with the back of your hands, with your elbow, with your knee, with your cheek. Put your object on top of your head. Walk it around the room.

Place it on your desk. Find something that you can draw with but do not usually use for drawing. Find something to draw on that you usually do not draw on (paper towels, tissue paper, wrapping paper, newspaper).

Now do not draw your object but draw something *about* it. Draw how it felt to the back of your hand. Draw its texture. Draw a feeling you got holding it. Draw the sound it made while rolling on the floor.

Lesson 9. Nature Collage

Materials: Wax paper (two 8″ x 10″ sheets per child), wax crayons, an iron, scissors, staples, construction paper.

Go for a walk and collect several natural things from the school grounds (leaves, grass, stems, small stones).

Place your items in some arrangement that is pleasing to you on one of your wax paper sheets. Use your scissors to scrape off bits of different colored crayon. Sprinkle the bits of color over your arrangement in a pattern that is pleasing to you.

Place the second sheet of wax paper over the entire arrangement. With a warm iron, press all of it together. The wax of the paper and the crayons will melt and hold the arrangement together.

Staple strips of construction paper along all four sides for added support. Hang it in a window so that the light can shine through it.

Variation

When the class is on a field trip to a park, a zoo, a beach, etc., have the children collect natural items in that environment to make a group collage. Each child arranges his items in relation to what others have to contribute. They can use a table, a bench, or some other defined area to hold their items. They have to work together to get the items in an arrangment that is pleasing to all.

Lesson 10. Shape and Color Walk

Go for a walk, paying particular attention to shapes and colors. Look for things that stand out in sharp contrast to each other—the smooth glass window in the rough stone wall, the rough bark of the tree and its smooth shiny leaves, a tiny black ant on white cement, bright sunlight, dark shadows.

Talk about shapes or colors seen that surprised you. Begin each sentence with "I." "I was surprised to see round drops of water still hanging on to thin blades of grass." "I saw three blackbirds in the blue sky." "I saw a cat come out of the shadows. At first I thought it was a black cat, but when it got in the sun, I saw it had many different colors on it."

Lesson 11. Texture Walk

Go for a walk, paying particular attention to the various textures that surround you.

Feel and handle as many different textures as you can.

Feel different textures while closing your eyes.

Be aware of how you feel as you touch and handle each item. Take time to feel it in different ways; stroke it, rub it, tap it.

As you change items be aware of how you feel about the new texture compared to the one just handled.

Be aware of your hands and how you feel when you are not touching anything.

Talk about what you felt that surprised you. Did something feel smoother or rougher than you expected? Softer or harder?

Variation

Take a sheet of paper and a soft crayon with you on your walk and do a texture rubbing picture.

Be aware of seeing the texture, feeling it, and then rubbing over it.

It is better to take the texture walk before doing this. Many textures may be overlooked when viewed with the task of rubbing them in mind. You can see many textures that you cannot feel or would not want to feel—the rough texture of a shingle roof, the silky slime left by a snail. There are textures that you might like to feel but cannot get in a rubbing: the soft fur of a rabbit, the bumps of a cyclone fence as you walk by it, the smooth surface of a puddle.

Lesson 12. Draw Your Partner

Materials: Pen or pencil and several sheets of paper.

Choose a partner.

Look at your partner. Put your pen down on your sheet of paper and begin to draw your partner. Do not lift your pen from the paper at any time until you are finished, and do not look at your paper. When both you and your partner are finished drawing, tell each other what happened. Talk about yourself and what happened to you, not about your drawing.

Take a new sheet of paper and do it again. Talk about anything new you discovered about yourself or your partner.

Look at the drawings you have done. Decide if they are mostly straight or mostly curved lines. This time do it again, using the opposite type of line as much as you can. Talk about what happened.

Now use either only straight or only curved lines and draw your partner again. This time you can lift your pen whenever you want to. Talk about what happened.

Begin again with a clean sheet of paper. Close your eyes. Draw yourself without lifting your pen from the paper. Be aware of what you are experiencing as you do the drawing. When you are finished drawing, talk about what happened.

If the class has difficulty getting started in a discussion, ask some leading questions: How do you feel about the size of your drawings? What were the surprises? What did you leave out?

How do you feel about what you left out? This type of question can be asked after any or all of the drawings.

Variation

Repeat the entire sequence having the children use the opposite hand. Focus the discussion on differences between the hands.

What did you see when using the opposite hand that you had not seen before? What were the discoveries, the surprises? Again, talk about what happened to you, and not the "outcome" of the drawing.

Lesson 13. Painting Poem

Choose a partner. Spend some free time together, just talking and being together. (Allow five to ten minutes.)

Now take a sheet of paper and, without paying attention to what your partner is doing, draw your partner as you see him.

Now share your drawings with each other.

Turn your drawings over, and on the back write the following:

Your partner's name.

Two words that describe him.

Three words to give action to him.

Four words to tell how you feel about him.

Your partner's name again.

Read your poem out loud to your partner, one at a time so the entire group can hear.

Share anything else you want to with your partner.

Discuss the entire exercise with the whole group.

Lesson 14. Group Pictures

Materials: A large sheet of paper (18″ x 24″), brushes of various sizes, paints, jars of water.

Close your eyes and think of a time when you were very happy. Think about how you were then, and how you felt.

Add as many details as you feel are needed to get them into a "happy" fantasy.

Now open your eyes and pick a color you feel represents that happy feeling. Start drawing with a brush that seems to be the right size and shape for that happiness. Let the memory of being happy direct the movement of the lines. Don't think about drawing anything, just think about being happy. Be aware of your lines and how you feel as you make them.

At my signal, go to another picture. Look at the new picture and be aware of how it makes you feel. Do not judge it, just look at it and be aware of your own feelings. Now begin to put those feelings on the paper. Again choose a color and a brush that represent your feelings now. Work on the paper in front of you as if it were your own. Add to it and change it as your feelings direct. Do not think of drawing something, just express what you are feeling now.

At my signal, go to another person's painting. Look at the new painting. Be aware of what you feel. Again, choose a color and a brush to represent that, and begin to work on that painting as if it were your own.

Now get the paper that was yours in the beginning. Look at your paper, keeping in touch with how you are feeling. Do not judge the work as good or bad. Just look at it and be aware of your feelings. Be aware of how you feel about what others have added to your work. How do you feel about having changed someone else's work?

Share any surprises.

Be careful to avoid making judgments in terms of an "art project" during this lesson. It is the experience and what the child discovers about his feelings while doing this that are important, not the final product. Help the child talk about how he *feels* about the product and not the product.

UNIT ELEVEN
Blindfolds

A baby freely and enthusiastically uses all his senses in order to learn about the world around him. Give him an object and he will get to know it thoroughly. He will feel it, taste it, shake it to see if it makes any sounds. But by the time a child reaches school age, he has learned otherwise. "Don't touch." "Don't put that in your mouth." By the time he is in school, he has become heavily dependent on his eyes for learning about his world. He has learned to ignore his other senses almost completely as sources of information. Traditional curricula tend to reinforce this restriction by emphasizing reading, writing, and arithmetic—primarily visual experiences.

In order to reintroduce the child to his other senses, it is necessary to reduce his dependency on his eyes. This may not be easy to do. When you first ask a child to close his eyes, you may encounter a great deal of resistance, related to his dependency on his eyes as his only way of knowing. A child who uses all his senses easily will not have much difficulty closing his eyes since he knows how to receive information from his other senses.

One way to allow the child to reduce his dependency on his eyes is to provide opportunities for him to experience his world while blindfolded. (You can either have the children bring scarves to tie over their eyes or make blindfolds for the class by cutting a piece of fabric-backed vinyl like a sleep mask and sewing elastic to the sides.)

Children are enthralled by wearing a blindfold at school. The child may be afraid to keep his eyes covered for very long without peeking, but he will keep wearing the blindfold and so increase the time he feels safe while blindfolded. He will develop a willingness to wear it for a longer time than he could manage to keep his eyes closed. By really removing his sight on his own terms, and for only as long as he is comfortable, the child becomes aware of seeing and brings new life and excitement to whatever work he does following wearing a blindfold.

Once the child can wear the blindfold comfortably for at least five minutes, he returns to old materials in the classroom with renewed interest. Blindfolds delight the child who learns best through tactile experiences. If he is blindfolded, he does not get questioned by other children for going back to materials that have been mastered visually, since they all know how difficult it is to do even familiar things when blindfolded. Many of the children will return to old puzzles and learn to do them again blindfolded. They will experiment with Cuisenaire rods in new ways. They will experience art materials—particularly clay—anew. Even dancing feels different when blindfolded. All lessons concerned with any of the five senses are intensified. By removing the use of his eyes, the child can concentrate more on touching, smelling, listening, or tasting. Even vision can be more intense if it has not been experienced for a while.

Objectives

To identify objects through senses other than sight.

To identify sounds without sight.

To identify odors without sight.

To experience taste sensations without sight.

To develop a new awareness of old familiar scenes by being in them without sight.

To develop the ability to receive information from all five senses.

Lesson 1. Free Exploration

Here is a blindfold for each one of you. What can you do with it?

Allow the children time to play with the blindfolds. Besides wearing it on their eyes, what else can they do with it? It can be worn as a hair band. It can be a sling for a "broken" arm. It can be worn around the neck as a decoration. After they have had some free time, bring the group together again.

Who can put his blindfold on correctly? When is it on correctly? (When you cannot see.) Who can walk from where he is to the other side of the room and back again? (Allow one child at a time to do so.) How do you walk when you are wearing a blindfold? How do you know where to go? What would you like to do with your blindfolds now? If possible, do it.

Don't be concerned if at first some children peek while wearing their blindfolds. However, praise and encourage those who allow themselves to move about without seeing. Allow time for free exploration. It may take some children a long time even to try on the blindfolds. At the end of this game, leave the blindfolds out and available for the children to play with during their free time, activity time, or recess.

Lesson 2. Passing Familiar Objects

Sit in a circle. Put your blindfold on. I am going to give each of you a familiar object from our classroom. You will have time to feel the object. When I make a sound, you are to pass it on to the child on your right and receive a new one from the child on your left.

Give each child an object from the room—scissors, paint brush, ball, pencil, etc. If there are several objects of the same kind—several pairs of scissors, for example—pass them out so that they are not all together, allowing the child to feel other objects before receiving scissors again. Use a sound, such as snapping your fingers, to signal them to pass their objects to the child on the right and receive a new one from the child on the left. Stand in the center of the circle to retrieve dropped and lost items. Don't wait so long that the children become discouraged and remove their blindfolds.

Encourage the children to go beyond just identifying the objects. Expand "This is a spoon" to "This is a spoon. It is hard and smooth. One end feels narrow and flat. The other end feels round and curved." Or "This is a stapler" to "This is a stapler. It can move. It feels rough here and smooth here."

Lesson 3. Passing Strange Objects

Repeat as in Lesson 2, except this time give the children items that have a special olfactory or tactile quality, such as whole cloves, fruits, flowers, scented candles, or bits of fabric, sandpaper, fur, and metal.

Encourage the children to keep their blindfolds on throughout the experience. This may be difficult for some. Assure them that it is all right not to know, not to be able to label what they have. Urge them to use their fingers, noses, mouths to know—at least for a while.

Leave all the objects out for the children to see and handle when the lesson is over.

Variation

Place the items to be passed in open boxes. This removes the sense of touch as well as the sense of sight. See how many items the child recognizes by the smell or the sound the item makes in the box.

Lesson 4. Eating

Prepare a bag with small bits of foods of different textures and tastes for each child. Select foods that are hard, soft, sweet, sour, crunchy, and mushy. For example: peanuts, raisins, chocolate chips, lemon drops, potato chips, prunes. It is important that all the items be dry; otherwise the tastes and textures will get mixed up.

Put your blindfold on. Eat the items in this bag, one at a time. Feel the item with your fingers before you chew it. Be aware of your tongue, your teeth, and your throat as you chew and swallow it. Pause a while before putting another item in your mouth.

What did you discover? Which things did you like to eat? What did you like about them? Which taste did you like most? Which texture did you like most?

You might wish to have extra amounts of all the foods so that the children can have more of the ones they liked best.

Lesson 5. Feel a Familiar Place

Take the class to a familiar place—it may be the school playground or a nearby park. Have each child wear a blindfold for as long as possible while attempting familiar activities. Do not insist that he keep the blindfold on. Let each child decide when he must use his eyes as well as his ears and hands to be able to be comfortable in his environment.

Encourage him to experience a variety of activities: swing

while blindfolded, go across traveling bars, run in an open space, feel sand or grass, go down a slide. For safety's sake, have one child do this blindfolded while another child watches him in order to warn him of any danger.

Try to get each child to wear the blindfold long enough to experience a newness of seeing when he takes it off.

Lesson 6. Blind Walk

When each child can wear a blindfold comfortably for at least five minutes, have him choose a partner. One puts on a blindfold, the other does the seeing for both of them. The seeing partner takes his blind partner for a walk, providing as many experiences along the way as possible.

The partners can do this anywhere, even in the classroom. However, the space and variety available outdoors obviously make it desirable to move outside if possible.

After about ten minutes, have the children change places. The one who was blind becomes the seeing partner, taking the other on a blind walk.

Allow time for a discussion at the end.

Which role did you prefer? Taking your partner, or being taken for a walk? Did anything special happen to you along the way? If you were to do it again, is there anything you would do differently?

Lesson 7. Blindfold Games

"Says who?"

Tap one child, who begins talking, saying anything but his name. The others guess who is talking.

Strange tastes

Give each child something small enough to put directly into his mouth—a peanut, a piece of popcorn, candy, a piece of carrot, celery, apple. Have the child tell what he ate without naming the item by describing its taste, sound, feel, etc. Have the others guess what he ate.

"What's that?"

Make a noise. The child who identifies it then makes a noise for the others to guess.

Blindman's bluff

Blindfold one child and have him move around in the group of children, identifying individuals through touch.

Still pond

Form groups of six to eight children. Each group forms a circle.

One person stands in the middle, wearing a blindfold.

The children on the outside of the circle move around until the center person calls "Still Pond."

The child in the middle finds a person and tries to identify him by touching his face and hands.

The person who was thus chosen then goes into the middle, and the game continues.

UNIT TWELVE
Sheets

In order to work with sheets in your classroom you need a double bed sheet for each child, a large space in which to work, and a great deal of stamina and courage.

The advantage of using sheets is that each child can have a place inside the class all to himself. He can use the sheet as a protective shield between himself and the eyes of his peers. A very shy, quiet child may let himself go while under the sheet —yelling and pushing—only to become placid once again upon removing the sheet. Other interesting things may also develop. A very aggressive, boisterous boy may refuse to leave the group to go under a sheet by himself. Or a child whom you had observed in many awkward movements may go through the life cycle of a plant with surprising grace and beauty, using his sheet to shield him from the eyes of others. In his own private world he can move in more fluid ways. A fearful little girl may crawl under her sheet, stay very still during an entire lesson, and then resist coming out and returning to the group. Two children who would not even look at each other in regular class periods end up being partners while under their sheets. From that they begin to see each other when sheets come off. Each child begins to let the other into his awareness, into his life.

The lessons in this book have been divided into units for the sake of convenience. In reality, many of them overlap each other, and the decision to put them into one unit or another was completely arbitrary. Each one adds something to and enriches the others. This unit, since it is the last, can be done as a final summarizing unit, or the lessons can be used in conjunction with the preceding units. Any of the preceding lessons will enrich these lessons with sheets—and sheet work will enrich the other lessons.

The effectiveness of sheet work depends on a great deal of imagination, self-awareness, other-awareness, and responding to nature. If the teacher and the child have shared experiences and have learned to relate to each other in other lessons in other units, and to bring to the classroom other life experiences, this will not be difficult.

If you do not force a child into doing a lesson, into going beyond his own inner limits, if you give him the right to be responsible for what he can and cannot do, the sheet lessons may be the most exciting of all to the child. You cannot know what is happening to him when he is covered with a sheet. It is not necessary for you to know in order to be his teacher.

The greatest times of all with the sheets come when the children are allowed to experiment and create with them on their own—at Halloween when they make up costumes, using the sheets as "rugs" in a make-believe bakery so that spilled flour will not show up, using a pile of sheets as a nest to lie on while reading. There is no way to predict how the children will use the sheets next if they are available to them.

Objectives

To provide the child with another way to relate to the here and now.

To expand the child's imagination.

To provide alternative ways of dealing with aggression.

To provide alternative ways to act out roles in nature.

To experience a new kind of space.

To provide alternative ways to create an artistic expression.
To review other experiences in this book in a new way.

Lesson 1. Then and There...
Here and Now

Spread your sheet out flat. Lie on top of it. Do not talk while you are lying there.

Look at all the other children here. When you feel like it, get under your sheet. Completely cover yourself.

Once you are covered, go somewhere in your imagination. Go wherever you want to go.

When you are ready, come back here, take your sheet off, and look around.

Then go under your sheet again.

Go away and come back when you feel like it.

Allow time for the children to establish their own rhythm of withdrawal and contact. Let them go away and come back several times.

When all, or nearly all, are back, ask them all to come back and stay here now.

Where did you go? How did you feel when you were there? How did you feel when you came back here? What are the differences between here and there?

Ask the children how things looked when they opened their eyes here. Were things in sharp focus, or were they fuzzy? Generally, if vision is sharp, they are in the here and now; if vision here is fuzzy, they are still in the then and there. There may be nothing you can do to make the child want to be in the here and now, but with this lesson at least you can know, and help him to know, that he is in the then and there.

Lesson 2. Being Alone Here and Now

Sit in a circle, not touching anyone.

Put your sheet over your head.

Now try to think of how you feel when no one wants you.

You know you are in a circle. When you feel like it, move away from the circle in slow motion.

Find a place to stop.

You are all alone. No one is near. Only you, the sheet, and the floor. Be completely alone for a while. (Allow no more than three minutes.)

Now lie down on the floor—still covered with your sheet.

Roll yourself up in your sheet as tightly as you can. Be very still. Feel the sheet all around you.

Now begin to roll around. If you roll into someone you may still wish to be alone. If so, move away. If you want to be close to someone, stay near whomever you touch.

Return to the circle.

Discuss what happened. How do you feel when you are alone? Did this remind you of a time when you were really alone? How did it feel to have other people touch you after you had been alone for a while?

Lesson 3. Dancing (Sensory Awareness)

Find a private space in the room.

Crawl under your sheet.

Listen to quiet music. Do not think of anything, but let thoughts and images come to you. Let your mind drift with the music. Let it go anywhere it wants. (Allow about fifteen minutes.)

Gradually come out from under your sheet. Take your

time. Don't talk. Meet one person at a time with only your eyes.

Slowly move to someone.

Join others until the whole group is together.

Play lively music.

Dance.

How did your mind and body respond to the music at first? (The quiet music.) What images came to you, what sensations did you have? What did you do with those sensations? How did your mind and body respond to the music that was played later? What images came to you, what sensations did you have? What did you do with those sensations?

Lesson 4. Imagination Game... Orange and Blue

Crawl under your sheet in a space of your own.

Imagine you are a ball.

Imagine you are either an orange or a blue ball.

Move around as an orange or a blue ball.

Make an orange or a blue ball sound to go with your movement.

If you are orange, try to find a blue ball. Dance with him.

If you are blue, find an orange ball and dance with him.

Find another ball to be with. See if you can discover what color he is by his sound and movement.

Find another one. Dance with him.

Join with other balls. Keep joining until you are all together, dancing.

Remove your sheets if and when you want to.

Lesson 5. Making Contact...Polarities

Completely cover yourself with your sheet. You cannot stand up. You can be on your hands and knees. You cannot talk.

Now imagine that you are either very large or very small.

Begin to move around that way. If you are large, move as if you are large. If you are small, move as if you are small. (Allow at least three minutes for movement.)

Now make a sound to go with your size.

Now, if you are large, try to find someone who is small who will stay with you and be your partner.

Once you find a partner, find a way that large and small can move together. Move to a space of your own. Continue to make your own individual sound.

Discover if the two of you can now make a sound together —make one sound instead of two separate sounds.

When you can move together and make a sound together, take your sheets off. See if you can continue to move together and make sounds together.

Now talk to each other about what you did.

If the group has a great deal of difficulty making contact, have them repeat the process several times before they take the sheets off and encounter one another face to face.

Lesson 6. Aggression Game

Get under your sheet. Remember the time when you were a baby, or think about a baby you know. Begin to move about on your hands and knees like a baby. Make sounds like a baby. Still staying under your sheet, meet other babies.

Talk to them with your baby sounds. You do not have words yet, but you do have sounds. Now find a space of your own.

Slowly take your sheet off, but still be a baby. Crawl around and meet other babies. Remember, you don't have any words, just sounds.

Now you learn your first word. It is "No." Keep crawling, meeting other babies. Talk to them using your one and only word. See how many different meanings you can give to the word by using it with different sounds, and by using it with different voice inflections.

Go to a space of your own again. Now imagine you are as old as you really are. Take some time to "grow up" and then come together as a group.

What did you discover? Was it easier to be a baby under your sheet or out of your sheet? How many different ways did you find to use the one word you had? How did you feel being a baby? What did you like about it, what didn't you like? How do you feel about being your own age now?

Lesson 7. More Aggression

Get under your sheet. Imagine you are a baby again. It can be you as a baby or a baby you know. Begin to crawl around and meet other babies. Today you are in a grumpy mood. You feel like pushing everything and everyone around. Push other babies around as you come into contact with them. Remember, you are a baby, and you can only push in ways a baby can push.

Now go to a space of your own. Be alone for a while. Remember how it felt to push others around as a baby. Now imagine you are about three years old. Get up on your knees to show that you have grown up somewhat. Move around on your knees. You are still in a grumpy mood though, so as you meet others, you want to push them around. Push them as a three-year-old would push. Now you become a tired three-year-old. Go to a space of your own and curl up in your sheet. Take a little rest. Since you are only three, you may even want to suck your thumb as you take a rest.

Now imagine you are still in a grumpy mood, but now you are as old as you really are. Walk around and meet other children who are in a grumpy mood. Do whatever you usually do when you are in a grumpy mood.

Now go to a space of your own again. Think about yourself now. How are you really feeling? Take your sheet off, and join the group.

Discuss what happened. How was your behavior now like your behavior when you were a baby? How was it different? Is it easier for you to be grumpy under a sheet than it is when you don't have a sheet on? In what other ways do you and other people hide grumpy behavior?

Lesson 8. Acting Out Nature

Use the sheets to act out a variety of scenes taken from nature.

Be a seed, with the sheet being the seed covering. "Grow" out of it. Use the sheet as a part of the growing plant—waving in the wind, blossoming, drying up, falling to the ground as the plant begins to die. Create a new seed. Then be the seed again, ready to grow next season.

Be a caterpillar egg inside the sheet. Grow out of it and become a tiny caterpillar by wrapping yourself in the sheet.

Be the caterpillar. Grow out of your skin several times.

Go into your sheet to be like the caterpillar in the chrysalis. Come out as a butterfly, using the sheet as your wings. Be the butterfly.

Be a bird's egg.
Hatch. Be a baby bird.
Grow.

Designate areas for migration, north and south. Have the birds migrate.

Make a nest with the sheet.
Be the egg again.

Lesson 9. Space

Get under your sheet. Close your eyes. Clear your mind of all thoughts, ideas, words. Take a few deep breaths. Just relax. Let yourself relax so that you seem to sink into the floor.

Now, still with your eyes closed, imagine that where you are now is your total space, your environment. Listen to the sounds around you. Smell the air as you breathe in. Feel it leave your body as you exhale. Feel the floor underneath you. Feel the sheet on top of you.

Now, slowly open your eyes. Begin to look around your space under the sheet. See where the sheet meets the floor. See it on parts of your body. Slowly you discover you can move your fingers, you hands, your arms. You can move your toes, ankles, legs. Slowly bring all their movements together so you can get up on your hands and knees. Watch how your movements affect the movements of your sheet, how they affect your space.

Slowly crawl around. Be aware of your space as you crawl. See how it changes. See what new things come into it as you move. Encounter other beings. Watch their effect on your space. Where do they push into your space? Where do you push into theirs?

Move into a space of your own. Slowly bring yourself to a standing position. Be aware of your entire body as you do so. What changes occur in your space as you stand up? Once you are standing, look again at the space you have created. Look at the sheet. Feel it on your body. Be aware of your breathing. Slowly begin to move about, being aware of the changes as you do so. You may meet others. Be aware of their effect on your space. Imagine your effect on their space.

Move to a space of your own. Slowly, slowly, remove your sheet. Be aware of the space around you now. Be aware of what you see and how you see it. Be aware of the smells. Be aware of how the air feels on your skin. Be aware of the sounds around you.

When you are ready, join the group.

This may be an intense experience for the children. If you experience them as being very quiet and withdrawn, don't be concerned. Let them go to a quiet activity. Give them some time and space. It may also be that they are excited after this experience. If so, let them talk about what they discovered. What were the surprises? What did they like about the lesson? What didn't they like?

Lesson 10. Art

Get under your sheet. Be by yourself for a while. Imagine that you are a work of art, but you are a part of a larger sculpture or picture. You need others to make you into a complete sculpture or picture. Experience different settings, different people. Experiment with different forms. Then settle on one. With another person or persons, form your sculpture or painting. When you think you have completed it, remove your sheet and look at your creation.

Talk about what you experienced.

If possible, have a Polaroid camera available for this lesson. Take pictures of the children before they remove their sheets.

Lesson 11. Paint Your Sheet

This should be done after the children have used the sheets many times, and only with sheets that are ready to be discarded.

Think about the times you have used these sheets. Think about the lessons you did with them. Think about the things you discovered about yourself and others while using the sheets.

You might wish to review the things they have experienced with their sheets.

Lay your sheet out flat and, using crayons or paint, draw pictures on your sheet to show what you experienced with it. You can draw a picture of something that happened, or you can make a design to symbolize what happened to you while using the sheet. If possible, use all of the sheet to show what happened to you.

If some children do not have sheets, let them work with someone who does.

Describe your drawing and your sheet experiences to someone in this group. Take your sheet home and describe it to someone at home.

3
A Confluent
Learning Experience

It is possible to develop confluent learning by integrating affective experience with the cognitive dimensions of learning. It is also possible to do it the other way around: by bringing cognitive dimensions into an affective experience. Up to now, the lessons in this book have all but ignored the cognitive domain. Here is one last lesson to illustrate how much cognitive material can be elicited from one affective lesson, and how even one affective experience can become a total curriculum by integrating the cognitive dimensions available from various subject areas.

THE ANGRY SOCK

Materials: One sock per child and material for stuffing the socks, e.g., beans, rice, sand, small pebbles.

Take your sock and, using the things you find here, stuff it. As you do so, think about all the times you get angry. Each time you put something into your sock, really stuff it in there, saying, "I get angry when . . ." Fill the sock with your anger. Stuff all your anger into the angry sock. Leave room enough at the top of your sock, the cuff part, to be able to tie a knot in it.

Double-check to be sure all socks are securely tied before going on.

Throw your angry sock in the air and catch it. Feel the weight of your anger. Throw your angry sock against the floor. Listen to the sound. Throw it against the wall. Listen to it again. Hit it with your hand. Feel your anger. What else would you like to do with your angry sock? If possible, do it.

Wait to see what the children do with their socks. It may or may not be necessary for you to set limits for the sake of safety. If you see the children engage in hazardous activities, stop them and make a few explicit rules: Don't hit anyone with a sock full of pebbles because it might hurt them. Don't throw your sock at the windows or lights because they might break.

It is best to do this lesson when you experience the class as needing a release for anger, at a time when they are difficult to live with and seem about to explode, when every little thing sets them off.

Here is how "The Angry Sock" lesson may be integrated into normal classroom subject areas.

Language Arts: The child can write about his experiences. He can read his story to another child. He can listen to other stories. He can use his story to work on spelling, diction, and grammar appropriate to his grade level. An advanced child can write a story from the sock's point of view. "I am an angry sock . . ." (One class coined the word "hardfast" while working with their angry socks. When you hit someone so as to hurt him, you give him a "hardfast." This led to further investigations into the origin of words.)

Math: Primary children can throw their socks and see which goes the farthest, which is the closest, which is the heaviest, which is the lightest, etc. Intermediate children can throw the socks and accurately measure the distances they traveled. Which sock went the farthest? What could account for that? Advanced children can estimate the number of beans it will take to fill their socks and check out their guesses.

Fill a small container with beans. Count the number of beans in it. Count the number of times the small container must be filled in order to fill the sock. Multiply the number in the small container by the number of times it is used to fill the sock, and that gives a close estimate of the number of beans in the sock.

Science: The children can be introduced to problems concerning weight, mass, and energy by throwing socks stuffed with different materials. They might also learn about the origin of the material of the sock as well as the material used to stuff it.

Art: The children can turn their angry socks into angry puppets. They can draw on them, paste facial features on them, and add yarn or string hair. They can then create a puppet theater and puppet plays to act out angry scenes.

They can draw pictures of angry faces, angry animals, angry skies, etc.

Social Studies: The socks can help to develop responsible citizens. "Who is angry?" "I am." "Who is hitting Johnny?" "I am." "What else can you hit?" "My angry sock." It can be used to help develop an awareness of others who share the same space and needs. "Don't hit me, I'm not your sock." A primary child can carry his sock around as if it were a pet if he is studying animals or a baby if he is studying families. He can hold it close to him during times of stress or fatigue. An advanced child can turn his sock into a voodoo doll upon reading about witchcraft in another culture.

Here is just a partial list of behavioral goals and objectives available from experiencing "The Angry Sock."

Language Arts: Talk about an experience using sentences beginning with "I."

Be able to listen to what others experience.

Write about an experience.

Read what others wrote about an experience.

Math: Be able to make comparisons of distances and weights.

Be able to record accurate measurements.

Be able to estimate a large number and check it out with counting and multiplication skills.

Science: Be able to define weight, mass, and energy in scientific terms.

Be able to translate experiments with weight, mass, and energy into a scientific formula.

Be able to describe things in terms of their weight, mass, and energy.

Be able to describe the origin of a material.

Art: Be able to represent anger in an artistic form, either through drawing or through making a puppet.

Become involved in creating a play.

Social Studies: Be able to express anger in a socially acceptable way.

Be able to express fatigue in a socially acceptable way.

Be able to role-play something from another culture.

Through this integration we can once again see that everything is connected, is part of a whole. Life is not compartmentalized. We experience life in its totality. We then impose order on our experiences so that we may assimilate what is important to us.

People are not compartmentalized, but until recently we have been teaching only one part of the living, functioning, working, interacting beings we know as children. They are more than just a brain. They are total beings, composed of mind and body, emotions, senses, and actions.

Most adults who have gone through our educational system have been taught to use only their minds, and only sometimes. Every human being, in order to mobilize the potential he already has available within himself, must above all be excited to be alive—willing to take risks, try new experiences, to be open, to be creative, to want to learn. He must have opportunities to experience his total being, to integrate his mind, and body with his emotions, senses, and actions.

The integrated person will love life, be aware of his feelings and his thoughts, be able to use freedom responsibly, and be the kind of person who can develop creative answers for the future.

Bibliography

BORTON, TERRY. *Reach, Touch and Teach*. New York: McGraw-Hill, 1970. A readable, provocative, informative introduction to the development of a curriculum aimed at dealing with students' concerns. Borton believes that major emphasis should be placed on helping children understand the process of change, giving them practice in using it, and allowing them to change themselves in their own ways. The book presents numerous examples of affective techniques as used in various projects throughout the country.

BROWN, GEORGE. *Human Teaching for Human Learning: An Introduction to Confluent Education*. New York: Viking, 1971. An account of the Ford Foundation–Esalen Institute project, containing a statement of the purposes of the project, extensive examples of affective techniques and their classroom applications, and a series of personal commentaries by teachers involved in the project. The sections on techniques and their applications are filled with practical suggestions for teachers who wish to experiment in confluent education.

DEMILLE, RICHARD. *Put Your Mother on the Ceiling: Children's Imagination Games*. New York: Walker, 1967. A delightful book which deals with children's fears and joys through imagination games. The introduction presents an excellent rationale for the deliberate expansion and development of imagination skills within the context of classroom learning. It also provides an exciting form that can be used by children in creative writing.

FAGEN, JOEN, and LEE SHEPHERD, eds. *Gestalt Therapy Now*. Palo Alto, Calif.: Science and Behavior Books, 1970. A useful collection of articles reporting new developments in the theory, techniques, and applications of Gestalt therapy. Of special interest to educators are "Anger and the Rocking Chair: Education of Emotionally Disturbed Children," by JANET LEDERMAN; "A Child with a Stomachache: Fusing Psychoanalytic and Gestalt Techniques," by RUTH C. COHN; and "Staff Training for a Day Care Center," by KATHERINE ENNIS and SANDRA MITCHELL.

GREER, MARY, and BONNIE RUBINSTEIN. *Will the Real Teacher Please Stand Up?: A Primer in Humanistic Education.* Pacific Palisades, Calif.: Goodyear Publishing Company, 1972. Presents excerpts from books and articles in humanistic education, from children's writings to statements by leaders in the field. It has questions and games for the reader to ponder and play. With this book as a guide, the reader can plan his own continuing reading program.

GUNTHER, BERNARD. *Sense Relaxation Below Your Mind.* New York: Collier Books, 1968. A beautiful book of poetry with accompanying pictures of exercises designed to relax and awaken the body, release the mind, and stimulate the senses. Many of the exercises can be used in the classroom, to relax or to stimulate the children.

JONES, RICHARD M. *Fantasy and Feeling in Education.* New York: New York University Press, 1968. Beginning with a perceptive critique of the Education Development Center's curriculum, "Man: A Course of Study," and focusing on its failure to deal with the students' emotions, Jones goes on to point out the importance of fantasy and creative thinking in education. He makes specific recommendations for new approaches to affective education. This book is difficult to read at times, but it is worth the effort for a theoretical base for affective education.

LEDERMAN, JANET. *Anger and the Rocking Chair: Gestalt Awareness with Children.* New York: McGraw-Hill, 1969. A dramatic, poetic account of the Gestalt methods of here and now and taking responsibility for one's self. Rather than suppress their anger, Mrs. Lederman helps her pupils to transform those powerful impulses into constructive attitudes and behavior.

LYON, HAROLD C., JR. *Learning to Feel—Feeling to Learn.* Columbus, Ohio: Charles E. Merrill, 1971. A compilation of ideas in the field of affective education from different people working in many different areas. The sections on "Humanistic Education Techniques" and "Applying Humanistics to Classroom Situations" are particularly valuable.

PERLS, FREDERICK. *Gestalt Therapy Verbatim*. LaFayette, Calif.: Real People Press, 1969. An informative and readable introduction to the theory and process of Gestalt therapy. The first 71 pages explore the theoretical basis; the rest of the book consists of verbatim transcripts of Gestalt therapy sessions.

ROGERS, CARL. *Freedom to Learn*. Columbus, Ohio: Charles E. Merrill, 1969. An excellent book which explains in detail how and why classrooms should be organized to free students to learn. Rogers clearly points the direction of education in the years to come.

SPOLIN, VIOLA. *Improvisation for the Theater*. Evanston, Ill.: Northwestern University Press, 1963. A popular text-manual on theater games, written primarily for the teacher. It contains more than 200 games and exercises, most of them designed to develop spontaneity and release creativity.

WEINSTEIN, GERALD, and MARIO D. FANTINI, eds. *Toward Humanistic Education: A Curriculum of Affect*. New York: Praeger Publishers, 1970. Describes and illustrates a "curriculum of affect," a model for teaching based on pupils' concerns and feelings rather than on purely cognitive goals, which relates to all children, whatever their age, socio-economic level, or cultural background. The chapters "Identity Education" and "Three Diagnostic Techniques" are of particular interest to the teacher seeking to deal with pupils' feelings and concerns.

TOWARD HUMANISTIC EDUCATION
A Curriculum of Affect

Edited by Gerald Weinstein and Mario D. Fantini

"*Toward Humanistic Education* is a courageous book, a timely reminder that all children have feelings all the time, in every experience; that they are not passive observers but bring their emotions into their learning; that learning proceeds most effectively when the feelings of the participants are recognized, accepted by the teachers, and permitted to play their natural roles."

—*Dr. Milton Senn*
Professor of Pediatrics and Psychiatry, Yale University

The "secret" of motivating the child to involve himself in the learning process—whatever his age, socio-economic level, or cultural background—is to deal in some way with the deep underlying feelings, wishes, and fears that stimulate his actions and color his response to the world.

This was the major finding of the Elementary School Teaching Project, an action-research program undertaken by the Ford Foundation's Fund for the Advancement of Education in an attempt to discover teaching practices that had proved successful with ghetto children. Spurred by this conclusion, the program staff turned its efforts to the development of a "curriculum of affect," a model for teaching based on pupils' concerns and feelings rather than on purely cognitive goals. By adapting this model, described and illustrated in this book, to suit his own competences and the needs of his students, the teacher can identify his pupils' concerns, use them in teaching standard intellectual content, or deal with them directly, as content in their own right. The model thus embodies an open-ended approach to teaching and learning that engages the child as a whole-hearted participant in the educational process by making that process "relevant" to him in the most profound sense.

PRAEGER PUBLISHERS
New York · Washington